Insight
Imagination
Individuality

Jyotika Panda

BLUEROSE PUBLISHERS
India | U.K.

Copyright © Jyotika Panda 2024

All rights reserved by author. No part of this publication may be reproduced, stored in a retrieval system or transmitted in any form or by any means, electronic, mechanical, photocopying, recording or otherwise, without the prior permission of the author. Although every precaution has been taken to verify the accuracy of the information contained herein, the publisher assumes no responsibility for any errors or omissions. No liability is assumed for damages that may result from the use of information contained within.

BlueRose Publishers takes no responsibility for any damages, losses, or liabilities that may arise from the use or misuse of the information, products, or services provided in this publication.

For permissions requests or inquiries regarding this publication, please contact:

BLUEROSE PUBLISHERS
www.BlueRoseONE.com
info@bluerosepublishers.com
+91 8882 898 898
+4407342408967

ISBN: 978-93-6261-035-5

Cover design: Shivam
Typesetting: Namrata Saini

First Edition: May 2024

Introduction

Welcome to the world of Vedic astrology, a place where ancient wisdom meets modern insight. I am a scholar and practitioner of Vedic astrology named Jyotika Panda. With a passion for scholarly inquiry, guide transformative journeys through celestial realms with reverence for ancient wisdom. Through rigorous study of sacred scriptures, I have discovered timeless principles governing the celestial dance of planets and stars.

As an astrological scholar, I aim to expand the boundaries of astrological knowledge by blending traditional wisdom with modern insights. To this end, I have researched various Vedic astrology branches, exploring intricate details of nakshatras and the profound symbolism of planetary combinations.

Astrology is a vast and intricate field, and embarking on its study can be a formidable task. When I first set foot in the world of astrology, I was met with numerous challenges. The multitude of dictums and the countless permutations and combinations were overwhelming. However, I persevered, focusing on the single house that is key to our daily lives.

The twelve houses are divided into three categories: Kendra and Trikona. The four most important houses, Kendra Pillars, represent the centre of the chart. On the other hand, the Trikona houses are the most powerful ones, where we cannot change anything. Upachaya House, in these houses, represents the areas of life where we will most likely experience success or failure due to our own doing.

However, we can rectify the issues in the Trik houses through our efforts. The Trik houses are the ones that provide us with an opportunity to change our destiny through self-improvement and hard work. Therefore, it is essential to understand the significance of these houses and make the most of them to lead a fulfilling life.

Come, join me on a journey of self-discovery and transformation. Let's explore the profound insights and timeless wisdom of Vedic astrology together. Allow the stars to guide us, and together, we'll illuminate the path to a brighter and more fulfilling future.

Let us delve together into the cosmic tapestry of existence, where the stars whisper secrets of the soul and planets offer guidance on our journey homeward. With an open heart and a curious mind, let's explore the limitless realms of Vedic astrology, where every chart tells a story, and every moment holds the promise of divine revelation.

May all be blessed with wisdom, insight, and the eternal light of truth on our journey together.

With sincere gratitude and divine blessings,

Jyotika Panda

E-mail- jyotika1079@gmail.com

Preface

Greetings, and welcome to the exploration of the Third House in Astrology. This expedition will divulge the profundity of insight, the domains of imagination, and the quintessence of individuality woven into the fabric of our cosmic blueprint. In this literature, we embark on a transformative odyssey through the celestial realm of the Third House, where communication, learning, and connections converge to shape the tapestry of our lives.

Astrology is a fascinating tool that allows us to delve into the depths of the human experience. By exploring the Third House, we can understand that communication involves more than just exchanging words; it is a sacred dance of insight where thoughts, ideas, and emotions intertwine to create a beautiful symphony of understanding.

Imagination is the driving force behind creativity and innovation and is the foundation of the Third House's realm. In this domain, we delve into the unlimited possibilities of the mind, where ideas flourish and dreams come to life. From a poet's pen to a scientist's laboratory, imagination shapes our perspective of the world and ignites the flames of discovery that illuminate the path towards knowledge.

Amidst the vastness of the cosmos, our individuality sets us apart as unique beings. Each of us has our own story to tell and our own truth to discover. In the Third House, we celebrate the diverse expressions of human experience, honouring the myriad ways we communicate, learn, and connect with the world and each other.

In the pages of this literature, we embark on a journey of self-discovery, guided by astrology's celestial wisdom and the potency of insight, imagination, and individualism. Together, we unravel the enigmas of the Third House and unlock the obscured depths of our inner selves, embracing the full range of our intellectual and social potential.

Dedication

With profound gratitude and reverence, I humbly dedicate this book to my beloved parents, whose unwavering love, guidance, and sacrifices have profoundly impacted every page of my journey. Their boundless support and encouragement have been a guiding light, providing me with the strength and conviction to pursue my aspirations. Additionally, I offer heartfelt homage to my revered Guru, whose wisdom has illuminated my path and enriched my soul. His profound influence has been instrumental in shaping not just my intellect, but also my character, and through his guidance, I have discovered the true essence of learning and growth. With deepest appreciation, I dedicate this work to you, my eternal source of inspiration.

Contents

Maa Saraswati Vandana...1

Pioneering the Pathway 2

Unveiling the house.. 9

Mental and Physical Vitality..13

Habits of Third House According to Zodiac................................... 21

Sahaja (Who was born together) Sibling..28

Power of inner potentiality.. 49

The power of name 115

Third house lord in different House.. 132

Dasha 144

Yoga Related to the third house..154

Disease-related to Gemini and Mercury.....................................157

Maa Saraswati Vandana

Yaa Kundendu tushaara haara-dhavalaa,
Yaa shubhra-vastra'avritaa,
Yaa veena-vara-danda-manditakara,
Yaa shweta padma'asana |
Yaa brahma'achyuta shankara prabhritibhir
Devai-sadaa Vanditaa,
Saa Maam Paatu Saraswati Bhagavatee
Nihshesha jaadya'apahaa ||

Who is pure white like Jasmine, with the coolness of the Moon, the brightness of Snow and shines like the garland of Pearls,

Who is covered with pure white garments,

Whose hands are adorned with Veena (a stringed musical instrument) and the boon-giving staff; and Who is seated on a pure white Lotus,

Who is always adored by Lord Brahma, Lord Vishnu, Lord *Shiva*, and other gods,

O Goddess Saraswati, please protect me and remove my ignorance completely.

Pioneering the Pathway

Have you ever considered the individual's efforts to shape one's life? It is amazing how much control we have over our destiny. Every decision and action we take contributes to our life's direction. So, what are some of the efforts you have made recently to shape your life in the way you want it to be? Just like by age three, A toddler works very hard to improve their walking, running, jumping, climbing, and hand skills and communicate effectively. In each competition, there are only three rewards. Third place is the bottom spot since one can go up or nowhere from here. like it's the last one. like how our actions can propel us upward or below, depending on our constant effort. The powerhouse of the entire zodiac house is the third house. it can make you or ruin you.

Just like a lighthouse serves various important functions such as guiding ships during poor visibility, warning them of potential dangers, aiding in the identification of ports and harbours, and ensuring the safety of sailors through search and rescue efforts, the third house (Tritiya Bhava) in one's natal chart plays a crucial role in providing guidance and direction in one's life. This house can be considered as the GPS of one's natal chart, helping to ensure safety and successful navigation through life's challenges by offering valuable insights into one's communication skills, relationships, siblings, and neighbourhood. It is a vital navigational tool that enables individuals to steer their lives in the right direction and avoid potential obstacles.

Natural Kalpurush Kundali: Gemini represents the third sign of the zodiac, symbolised by twins, and embodied by the divine creative activity. This creative force operates through the polarisation of spirit and matter. The symbol signifies the duality of the Gemini sign, which is the foundation of its significance in astrology. The divine creative activity is a powerful force that drives the manifestation of material reality, and the polarity of spirit and matter is the key to its operation.

In ancient times, a cosmic disturbance threatened the universe's balance. The gods were alarmed by this disruption and decided to seek the help of Lord Shiva, the Supreme Deity known for his immense power and wisdom. As the protector and sustainer of the cosmos, Shiva undertook a mission to restore harmony and order. During his journey, Shiva came across a powerful demon named Andhaka who had caused chaos through his evil deeds. Shiva fought bravely in the intense battle that followed, using his martial skills and divine weapons.

Andhaka, who possessed exceptional strength and resilience, was a formidable opponent. Shiva realised that defeating him would require an unconventional approach transcending brute force and aggression.

In a moment of divine insight, Lord Shiva invoked the feminine aspect of his being, the nurturing and compassionate energy of Goddess Parvati. She resided within him as his divine consort. Lord Shiva fused his essence with Parvati's by channelling this feminine power, merging their forms into a singular entity of unparalleled harmony and balance.

As a result, Ardhanarishvara, the half-male, half-female manifestation of Lord Shiva was born. With the combined strength of both Shiva and Parvati, Ardhanarishvara subdued the demon Andhaka, restoring peace and order to the cosmos.

It's truly fascinating how Shiva's transformation into Ardhanarishvara represents the inseparable unity of masculine and feminine energies within the divine, and how it inspires us to transcend dualities such as good and evil, creation and destruction. It is a beautiful reminder of the inherent harmony and balance that underlie all existence, and it can inspire us to seek unity and wholeness in our spiritual journey.

In Gemini, the symbol is a man with a club and a woman with a lute in her hand. The cause is Vayu and Guna, which is Sattva. The lord is Mercury. The term "dual sign" is often associated with the zodiac sign Gemini because it is believed to have two-fold meanings and a double purpose. All sorts of artistic qualities belong to these signs. It demands consistent efforts in one and all. This is the place for singers, dancers, all sorts of amusement, playing all games, gambling, house of upadesa, and social meetings. The Tattva of this house is Vayu(air). From where one's imagination originates. "Imagination reveals the gateway to one's life." Have you ever noticed how before cooking a delicious meal, we all gather various ingredients? It is like a treasure hunt, searching for the perfect combination of

Flavors to bring our recipe to life. It is amazing how the simple act of combining different ingredients can create such a wonderful culinary experience! The art of cooking, tailoring, playing, singing, engaging in different adventures, communicating, painting, driving, and writing stories - all require the use of one's hands as tools to transform abstract ideas and concepts into wonderful creations. These activities stimulate innovation, encourage self-expression, and lead to personal fulfilment.

The joint name "Gemini" indicates the inseparableness of the duality in men. It represents the outflow of the divine force that causes polarization in men, enabling the d According to the Hindu Puranas, Brahma created time, space, and a group of Archangels called Sadaka Purushas to carry out divine commands after the Trinity was established during cosmogenesis. However, this did not lead to the multiplication of the world. As a result, Brahma divided himself into male and female, whose union gave rise to Swayambhu Manu, the self-created Purusha, and SathaRapa, the hundred-faced female. Their union created the entire human family. This narration is similar to the biblical story of Adam and Eve, where Eve was created from Adam's rib and their union gave birth to the entire human brotherhood. Vine drama of human manifestation whose every fibre is woven with spirit and matter to occur.

Gemini represents the divine potential for creativity but embodies a duality between spiritual ascent and material descent. This duality allows for unlimited possibilities.

Gemini is characterised by conflict and instability and lacks contentment, satisfaction, stability, and tranquillity. The

Gemini individual will always be restless, searching for something that does not exist. Their heart will always be pursuing a mirage, causing instability. They will constantly be torn between conflicting loyalties, ideologies, demands, memories, and aspirations. Life may not be intense for them, and they may find prolonged periods of disinterest in life boring, making others perceive them as fickle and incapable of deep friendships.

When Swetaketu sought spiritual guidance from Yama, the Lord of Death, he selected the best guide for the task. Similarly, the inscrutable life of a Gemini is their best guide for spiritual unfoldment. Until the meaning of life is revealed to them, a Gemini individual will continue to confront death in its many forms. However, once the mystery is solved, Yama has completed his mission. This is why a Geminian is often in an intense mood of contemplation and brooding over life experiences, seeking to discover their meaning. They may experience depression, suicidal tendencies, thirst for greater indulgences and more excitement and experiences, but these will relate to the discovery of the meaning and purpose of life. Such events occur with a purpose, as Gemini must teach its disciples the mystery of life and death. They are very active on the subjective plane. One may find them attempting to use spiritual means to achieve material objectives or vice versa. They may be fascinated by spiritual healing.

It is known as Yuga, a term that does not translate perfectly to duration, but it does reveal something important about the sign. Many aspects of life may unfold for a Gemini, but the individuals themselves will remain unperturbed as if nothing momentous has occurred. However, deep-rooted impressions will be made on the psyche. Gemini is said to have strength at night, when the psyche is vitally active, and to be blind at mid-day when the turmoil of life is at its highest. This is why the sign tends to be more active in thoughts and feelings than objective physical actions. Despite their spiritual and psychic potential, Gemini is primarily a material sign, often associated with the merchant class. They enjoy gambling, pleasure haunts, dancing, and music, as well as sensuous pleasures and females. Gemini individuals think of spiritual heights but often indulge in physical and sensuous pleasures.

This is a sign that has great spiritual and psychic potential. However, it is primarily considered a material sign due to its association with the merchant class. Gemini is often linked to places of entertainment such as gambling houses, dancing and music floors, and pleasure haunts. The sign is associated with sensuous pleasures, females, music, and poetry. Despite the tendency of these individuals to think about spiritual heights, they often indulge in physical and sensuous pleasures. Sometimes, the opposite happens as well. When examining the relationship between the various planets that affect Gemini, we can see problems and pitfalls. However, Mercury and Jupiter, being lords of angels, are very powerful for Gemini ascendants. Their benefic rays are essential for integrating the polarisation of the Gemini personality, which is otherwise more likely to indulge in physical and sensuous pleasures. By integrating the easily excitable, quick, silvery mind with Jupiterian wisdom, discontentment can be eliminated, and tranquillity can be achieved.

The individual described possesses a commendable level of personality integrity, which allows them to effectively engage in repetitive daily business tasks, handle administrative details easily, and work cooperatively as part of a team. They are naturally inclined towards social interactions with their siblings, cousins, work colleagues, neighbours, and other community members. They are adept at handling small-scale administrative tasks that involve shared small-group concerns.

Unveiling the house

• Initiation • Imagination • Courageous/valour • Subconscious mind • Hobby • Telecommunicating device • Television, Visualisation • Mental health • Passion • Radio, Lighthouse, Metrology office • Daily routine journey, work • Subordinate in the work field. • Sibling, neighbourhood • Kith and kin • Writing, ability to think beyond • Art and paint, ink	• Job Interview • Name, Admit card, identity card • Order of sibling : First younger sibling 5th, second sibling 7th, third sibling 9th house • Body Part: Ear, Hands, arms, Neck, Throat, Thyroid gland, Chest, Upper Libs, Shoulder • Age : 3rd, 15th, 27th, 39th, 51st, 63rd, 75th, 87th • Animal: Birds like sparrow, pigeon, parrot, owl, hummingbird, falcon, cookoo • Swift moving animal: fox, squirrel, Monkey, Deer, swan, Hen, bee • Plants: Gooseberry, Moneyplant, Aloevera, Licorice, Basil, Rosemary, mint, • Chamomiles , sage ,lavender

- Gym, stadium, garden, playground
- Media, publishing house, Opera house, Theatre
- Bar, Pub
- publicity and advertisement
- conversation
- announcements
- declarations and documentation,
- media-messaging, whatsup, WeChat,insta, facebook,twitter,koo
- cinema, radio-television-internet,
- books-magazines-journals-blogs,
- travel itineraries, scheduling, schematics, planning,
- meetings,
- hand-craft, tool-use, technology.
- sibling-cousin-schoolmate-neighbour communications
- Ears and Hearing	- Spices : Green moong pulses,
- Places: Entry gateway of home
- Microscopic chart related 3rd house: Dreshkena(D3),Chaturvimshamsa (D24)
- Direction Of third house North North west
- Direction of Gemini: NNW

• Meetings • Mentality • Works with hand, including scripture and painting. • Orator,singer,dancer, delivering	

- Having a planet in the third house is always connected to one's fortune since it influences the ninth house.
- A malefic planet placed in the third house of a horoscope can give better results than a benefic planet.
- "Malefic planets accept the challenges that life provides, and as a result, individuals become more courageous in taking risks. The level of risk-taking capability is higher than that of the benefic planets posited in the third house. It is important to strive hard and fight for what you want, as it helps to build a sense of achievement."
- Having a benefic planet in the third house can enhance imagination and provide success within a timely manner, as long as there are no afflictions from planets in the ninth house.
- When a planet is in the third house, it influences certain behaviours. For instance, the moon may encourage singing, Mars may lead to sports, Venus may inspire painting, and Mercury may foster writing and language skills. Ketu may encourage interest in

occultism, tantra, and coding, while Rahu may inspire a passion for media, publicity, and technology.

- "When the Third house in a person's astrology chart is afflicted, it may cause them to change their place of residence frequently.".
- If the lord of the Third house, which is a natural benefic, is positioned in the 2nd house in a lady's chart, it may indicate wearing jewellery related to the 3rd house on the ear, hand, and neck.
- Whenever Jupiter is hemmed between mar and mercury, there is a black spot in the back.
- In Prasna Kundali, the third house and third lord can reveal the question of the querier.

Mental and Physical Vitality

"A bird sitting on a tree is never afraid of the branch breaking, because its trust is not on the branch but in its ability to fly."

The third house of one's natal chart is known to confer much about one's state of mind. It is believed that the strength of mental capability, courage, stamina, willpower, and proficiency in communication, writing, singing, and writing lyrics, all come from this powerful house. Additionally, one's artistic skills and hobbies are said to be associated with this house. The ability to endure the ups and downs of life is also believed to come from the third house of horoscope, which is represented by the significator of that house, Mars. It is also considered the first multrikon house from the 11th house of the elder brother, which is why it represents one's younger sibling as well.

If Mars, Saturn, or Venus is posited either in the third house or in the eleventh house (left hand), the individual is believed to be using a tambourine, among other instruments. Moreover, one's voice is also believed to depend on the planet in the third house. For instance, the Sun in the third house is considered authoritative, Mars is considered like the commander in chief, Mercury is considered childlike, Venus is considered melodious, Moon is associated with sweetness, Jupiter is like a temple priest,

Rahu is believed to produce a very high pitch tone, and Saturn is associated with a slow and sad voice.

It is also believed that one's conscience will help to get along with oneself. Goddess Saraswati is known as the only Goddess having the most melodious Veena held in her hands, while the swan is the logo of Saraswati. Lord Krishna is known for his melodious tune in the Flute made of bamboo, which enthralled not only Gopis but also all the creations of God. Mighty King Ravana pleased Lord Shiva only by reciting Sama Veda, which has its own peculiar rhythm, tune, and melody. In the early sixties, the Beatles introduced pop-songs in the music world in the West.

Astrologically, the affliction to the 3rd house is believed to result in an evil mind. The influence of Sun, Moon, Jupiter, Mercury, and Venus is believed to make one a singer, writer, poet, or musician. Jupiter is said to represent the higher attributes of man, such as aspiration, devotion, religion, spirituality, philanthropy, benevolence, sympathy, and brotherhood. His mission is to scallion suds of songs, joy, and place.

Moreover, the influence of other planets in the music world may be described as follows: Moon is believed to give a taste for instrumental music, Venus posited in voice signs (Gemini, Libra, Aquarius, Virgo, and Sagittarius) or in the second or third house is said to produce vocal musicians, Neptune is said to represent stringed instruments, and Mercury in earthy signs (Taurus, Virgo, Capricorn) is believed to represent Mridangam, whereas, in other signs, it is associated with Tabla (an instrument mostly played by Indian musicians with both hands).

It is also believed that singers should be free from stage fear. Astrologically, if the Moon, Mercury, or Jupiter does not have the contact or aspect of Mars, then the individual is believed to be filled with a fear complex. Saturn, being a depressor, is believed to cause inferiority complexes and fear complexes in people with the Moon and Mercury affiliated with Saturn.

Aries people tend to have a dynamic and direct approach to communication, which is reflected in their third house placement. They are often bold and commanding in their speech and may engage in regular business or commercial travel. Aries individuals often excel in journalism, media promotion, and project management. However, they can easily become bored and are always on the lookout for new challenges in their work. One potential downside for Aries is a lack of patience, which can sometimes manifest as impatience or frustration.

Aries: DON'T TALK, ACT

    DON'T SAY, SHOW

    DON'T PROMISE, PROVE

As Taurus is the third house, individuals born under this sign tend to have great relationships with their colleagues and younger siblings. They can be quite stubborn in their ideas and often express themselves in creative ways. It's recommended to only travel if it's absolutely necessary. They also tend to take breaks from their routine work and plan vacations to refresh themselves.

Taurus: "Laughter is brightest in the place where food is good." Irish Proverb

Gemini individuals are associated with the third house and have a natural curiosity to learn about various subjects. They possess superior imagination and intelligence and are skilled at writing and communicating effectively. They enjoy talk shows, documentaries, and humorous programs and love to travel to explore new things. However, they tend to hesitate when it comes to making long-term commitments. One of their negative traits is that they tend to speak before thinking and may not be the best listeners. They are also busy multitasking most of the time.

Gemini: "If the freedom of speech is taken away,

then dumb and silent, we may be led,

like sheep to the slaughter." By George Washington

The placement of Cancer in the third house suggests that one's mental habits and creativity will go through cycles of ups and downs throughout life. In this position, the individual is not interested in winning debates but rather seeks emotional validation. They have a natural aptitude for palm reading, hands-on healing like therapy, reiki, and dermatology. They also tend to defend and protect their siblings, friends, and teammates.

Cancer: "Man lives consciously for himself,

but serves as an unconscious instrument for the achievement of historical, universally human goals." By Leo Tolstoy

Leo being in the third house is associated with an independent mind, courage, proactivity, and rationality. They have innate and self-reflective thinking which makes them thoughtful and introspective. They prefer to be the center of attention in meetings, conferences, and group discussions and often dominate the conversation due to their personal brilliance. Leos possess a tremendous capacity to handle administrative management in the workplace.

Leo: "you were born to fit in,

but I was born to be stand out." Dr,Seuss

As per astrological beliefs, Virgo is associated with the third house, which is said to give individuals a structured mind. People born under this sign tend to have a detailed and categorical writing style and are inclined to organize their daily schedules for even the simplest of tasks. They are skilled in business administration, narration, and media production. Although usually soft-spoken, they can be critical of others from time to time and may display a bit of a funky attitude.

Virgo: "They say that nobody is perfect.

Then they tell you practice makes perfect.

I Wish they'd make up their mind." By David J Yarbrough

One with Libra in the third house has a composed mind, is a skilled negotiator, favors teamwork and social event organizing, and builds a favorable, cooperative group of business associates through balanced mental and communicative interactions.

Libra: "Life is like riding bicycle.

To keep your balance,

you must keep moving." By Albert Einstein

Scorpios who have their third house in their birth chart tend to be mentally restless and anxious individuals. They are often occupied with their thoughts but find it difficult to express them easily. Many times, they tend to be introverted and may fumble while speaking. They struggle with making even simple decisions due to their indecisive nature, which can also lead to low self-confidence. Scorpios with this placement tend to be secretive about their thoughts and ideas, but their appearance in daily life is quite mundane.

Scorpio : "We should ask God to increase our hope when it is small,

awaken it when it is dormant,

confirm it when it is wavering,

strengthen it when it is weak, and

 raise it up when it is overthrown." By john Calvin

Sagittarius is ruled by the Third House and is known to be independent, courageous, and optimistic. They are like born to be a teacher with broad and expansive mental gestures. They love guiding and coaching others and always talk related to rules and regulations. However, their attention to administrative details may get distracted by higher concepts.

Sagittarius : "Principles are guideline for human conduct,

> That is proven to have enduring, permanent value."
> *Stephen R. Covey*

As Capricorn is the ruler of the Third House, people born under this zodiac sign tend to have a thinking process that is inclined towards negativity. They often worry and imagine worst-case scenarios and are always checking to see how theoretical ideas can be put into practice. While they are calm and composed by nature, they may feel uncomfortable in crowded places. They are down-to-earth, sober, and speak in a calm manner. A quote that sums up their approach to life could be, "Hope for the best, but prepare for the worst."

Capricorn:" I put my heart and my soul into my work, and have lost my mind in the process." By Vincent Van Gogh

Aquarius, being the third house, can cause the individual to become mentally rigid and dogmatic. Their thinking process is usually abstract and driven by principles and theories that they have adopted due to a deep passion for scientific inquiry and a radical rejection of conventional theories. Sometimes, irrational thoughts may waver in their mind.

Aquarius: "when I examine myself and my methods of thought,

    I come to the conclusion that the gift of fantasy.

    has meant more to me than any talent for

    abstract positive thinking."Albert Einstein

Pisces are individuals who believe strongly in the third house, have visionary thinking, and are often drawn towards charitable perspectives. They often experience dream interpretation, meditation, and mental communication and have the ability to perceive emotional or psychic energy that is imperceptible.

Pisces : All our dreams can come true, if we have the courage to pursue them. By Walt Disney

Habits of Third House According to Zodiac

Habits are actions we tend to perform automatically in response to our surroundings. Such actions are often deeply ingrained in our behaviour and can significantly impact our daily lives. In astrology, the third house is considered the manager of habit formation. The sign and lord of the third house play a crucial role in shaping the habits we develop over time. Understanding the influence of the third house can give us insights into our habitual tendencies and help us take steps towards breaking negative patterns and cultivating positive ones.

Below the Third house in different zodiac signs:

Aries is in the Third House /Aquarius Ascendant. To achieve personal growth and improvement, it may be helpful for those with an Aries sign to consider making positive changes to their habits. Individuals tend to use profanity repeatedly to emphasise the validity of their opinions.

These individuals are known to be action-oriented and impulsive regarding work. They tend to dive into tasks without much analysis or forethought. They can start a project based on just an idea or inspiration. While this approach can lead to quick progress, it can also result in oversights and mistakes, making it both an advantage and a disadvantage.

Obstacle: People born under the Aries sign, being in the third house, are known for their tendency to interrupt others when they speak, which can often lead to frustration.

These individuals may twirl their hair during meetings or in a group setting, which can make a negative impression on others.

Taurus Being the third house/Pisces Ascendant.

Immediately say no – One of the worst habits of Taurus people is to refuse immediately. Say anything to them, they are never ready for it and say no without thinking.

Often busy shopping- Taurus people are often busy shopping. They are very extravagant.

Teeth grinding- One of the worst habits of Taurus people is their frequent gnashing of teeth. Due to this habit, they become the subject of everyone's discussion in any good or bad situation.

Very strict- Taurus people are often very stubborn as nature like a bull.

Do not like change- Taurus people do not like change. They refuse change outright or are not ready from within.

Gemini Being Third House/Aries Ascendant: Talkative

Gemini people are adept at gossiping. They never need a subject to talk about.

Busy on the phone—No matter how many important meetings you are sitting in, Gemini people keep checking their phones again and again. This habit often gets them irritated.

Not on one decision - Gemini people never stick to any one decision. They keep themselves confused and keep confusing others too.

Bored very quickly - Gemini people get bored very quickly. They often do not stay fixed in one place.t stay fixed in one place.

Cancer being Third house/Taurus Ascendant.

"Very emotional" is a cancer sign that people get emotional over talk. Due to this habit, many people keep distance from them.

"A lot of TV watchers"—Cancer people are very much into watching TV or mobile videos. Even when they are conversing in a group, their eyes are more on their mobile screens.

Complaints - Cancer signs people often complain about. Chaotic things can make them very angry.

Cancer individuals often appreciate antique items, but their curiosity about them can sometimes be intrusive to hosts when they visit their homes.

Leo being the third house /Gemini Ascendant – humorous and authoritative.

To scare people - Leo people often have this habit of keeping people intimidated. It can be difficult for them to miss and intimidate people every time.

Taking everything personally - Leo people take everything personally. Due to this habit, many people start distancing themselves from them.

No attention to look—Leo people do not pay any attention to their looks. They wear nice clothes but are unaware of when and where to wear them. Because of this, they often become a laughingstock.

Online Oversharing - Leo people do a lot of online oversharing. They often like to post a lot of personal photographs along with personal details on social media. Due to this, they may also have to suffer loss.

Virgo being Third house/Cancer ascendant- Keep giving unnecessary advice

Virgo people are often ready to give advice. Many times, people start distancing themselves from them due to this habit of theirs.

Avoidance—Virgos are experts at postponing things. Because of this habit, people start shying away from giving them any responsibility.

Unnecessary worry - Virgo sign people often worry unnecessarily. Their family members are often troubled by this habit of theirs.

Negative thoughts—Virgo signs people have very negative thoughts. They are often not very keen on new things. Sometimes, they become so sure that their positive thoughts never come true.

Libra, being third house / Leo Ascendent- falls in love without thinking.

Fall in love instantly- Libra people often fall in love instantly. Due to this habit, they sometimes cheat.

Over-possessive—Libra sign people are overly possessive about their things. They are balanced but do not believe in sharing.

Expensive—Like Taurus, People of the Libra zodiac are very expensive. They are so extravagant that sometimes they have two things in common.

Keepers of people's happiness—Librans often keep people's lives happy. However, they sometimes harm others in the pursuit of pleasing themselves.

Scorpio being third house/Virgo Ascendent - Too much expectation from others.

Mysterious- Scorpio people are very mysterious. They never allow their truth to be revealed in front of anyone.

High Expectations—Scorpions have high expectations from others. They never fulfil someone else's expectations, but they want others to fulfil their expectations.

Fear of spreading- Scorpio people have so much fear of spreading that they sometimes do not come out of their comfort zone due to fear. This habit of theirs sometimes becomes harmful to them.

Empowered—Scorpions are often the ones who exercise authority over other people. While making friends, they take utmost care that people remain under their control.

Sagittarius being third house/Libra Ascendent – Haste too much

No patience- Sagittarius people are very hasty. They expect instant results while doing any work.

Promise breakers—Sagittarius people are adept at breaking promises. They often make such promises that they are not even able to fulfil.

Too much work- Sagittarius people often stay late in the office. They also work, but their habit becomes trouble for others.

Wrong Explanators- Sagittarius people often explain their points in the wrong way. Sometimes, they say that they do not even have the intention to say.

Capricorn, being the third house/Scorpio Ascendant- remains immersed in thoughts.

Living in himself- Capricorn people are often immersed in thinking. They suddenly get lost in their thoughts while talking.

Critics – Capricorn people do not hesitate to criticise themselves or others.

Fear of going wrong—Capricorn people often start some work but fear going wrong, which confuses others.

Drink Habit—Capricorn people do not need only to drink alcoholic drinks; it is a minor habit for them to make a habit of coffee or tea, too.

Aquarius being third house/Sagittarius Ascendent – Means more than the life of others.

Means more than others- Aquarius people mean more to others than themselves. They are always curious to know who is doing what.

Sports and Playground- Aquarius people are very busy playing in the playground or playing online games. Because of this many times, their target remains incomplete.

Comfort Preferred—Aquarius people are comfort favourites. They postpone work for tomorrow, which harms them and others.

Pisces being the third house/Capricorn Ascendant– Day Dreamer

Daydreamer—Pisces sign people are often daydreamers. They live in their imaginations and suffer for this.

Commitment breakers- Pisces people are often the ones who break their commitments. For them, it is not a big issue.

Imposing their choice on others—Often, they impose their choice on others. Whether going to a theatre or a restaurant, they go to places of their own choice and never try a new one.

Living in the comfort zone- Pisces people do not want to leave their comfort zone. They never try any new work. Working hard is not even their thing.

Sahaja (Who was born together) Sibling

In Greek mythology, the constellation Gemini is associated with the twin brothers Castor and Pollux. Their story is one of brotherly love, loyalty, and adventure. According to legend, Castor and Pollux were born to different fathers. Castor was the mortal son of King Tyndareus of Sparta, while Pollux was the immortal son of Zeus, the king of the gods, who had seduced their mother, Leda, in the form of a swan. Despite their different parentage, the brothers were inseparable and shared a deep bond.

Castor was known for his exceptional skill in horseback riding and his prowess in battle, while Pollux was celebrated for his strength and bravery. Together, they embarked on numerous adventures, joining the Argonauts in their quest for the Golden Fleece and participating in the famous Calydonian Boar Hunt.

One of the most famous stories about Castor and Pollux involves Castor being fatally injured during a feud. Pollux was devastated by the thought of losing his brother and prayed to Zeus, begging him to grant them both immortalities. Zeus was moved by Pollux's devotion and transformed them into the constellation Gemini. From then on, they were placed side by side in the sky, where they remained together for all eternity.

In Greek mythology, Gemini's constellation symbolizes brotherly love, companionship, and the enduring bond between siblings. Castor and Pollux became the patron saints of sailors, who believed that their presence in the night sky brought protection and good fortune during voyages. Their story serves as a reminder of the power of love and loyalty, even in the face of adversity.

It is heartwarming to know that the beautiful city of Ayodhya was blessed with not just one but four amazing sons of Dasharatha—Rama, Lakshmana, Bharata, and Shatrughna. Rama and Lakshmana shared an incredibly close bond, with Lakshmana showing his unwavering devotion by always serving and protecting his elder brother, Rama. It is truly inspiring to see such a strong bond between siblings.

Rama's fourteen-year exile to the forest is the story's primary focus. This was ordered by his father, Dasharatha, as he made a promise to Rama's stepmother, Kaikeyi. Lakshmana, who was deeply attached to Rama, willingly accompanied him into exile. This meant leaving behind his wife, family, and the comforts of the palace. During their exile, Rama, Lakshmana, and Sita went through a lot of challenges and met quite a few interesting characters, including demons, sages, and allies. But there was something special about Lakshmana's unwavering devotion and support towards Rama throughout their journey. It is like he was the ultimate wingman! Their journey highlights the depth of sibling love and loyalty, which is so heartwarming to see Ultimately, the story culminates in the great battle between Rama and the demon king Ravana, who abducted Sita. With the help of Lakshmana and other allies, Rama defeats Ravana and rescues Sita, thus fulfilling his duty as a husband and prince".

The tale of Rama, Lakshmana, and Sita exemplifies the themes of sibling loyalty, sacrifice, and devotion, which are central to many Puranic stories. It emphasizes the importance of familial bonds and the virtues of righteousness, duty, and honour the characters uphold in their journey through life's trials and tribulations.

According to the principles of Kalpurusha Kundali, the zodiac sign Gemini represents the natural Third house. In astrology, the Third house is associated with younger siblings, communication, and short-distance travel. The Karaka or significator of the Third house is the planet Mars, which rules over courage, action, and energy.

No sibling:

As per the Brihat Parashara Hora Shastra (BPHS), any insights gained from analysing the Third house can also be applied to the third house from Mars. This means that by examining the position and aspects of the planet Mars in one's birth chart, one can gain further insights into matters related to younger siblings, communication, and short-distance travel.

If the third house lord in a natal chart is in a debilitated state or the third house contains Ketu or a debilitated planet, then one can infer that the person in question is likely to be the youngest among their siblings.

Number Of siblings: The number of siblings one may have can be indicated by the presence of planets in the third house. This is connected to the third house lord with Mercury and the strength of Mars.

Nature of Sibling: The nature and characteristics of siblings can be determined by analysing the ruling planet of the third house and any planets placed therein.

Relationship with siblings: Planetary aspects of the third house or its ruling planet can indicate the relationship quality with siblings.

Nature of Elder Sibling: The ninth house and connection between Jupiter, related to the first house, and its ruling planet can indicate the nature and influence of older siblings.

Education Of siblings: The overall condition of the third house and its ruler can indicate siblings' education.

Travelling with siblings: When the third house is favourably placed, it indicates enjoyable travel experiences with siblings.

Communication with siblings: The position of Mercury in the birth chart can indicate the quality of communication with siblings.

Inheritance and joint property: Inheritance matters involving siblings may be indicated by connections with mars between the third and fourth houses, such as joint ownership or inheritance.

Ch 1

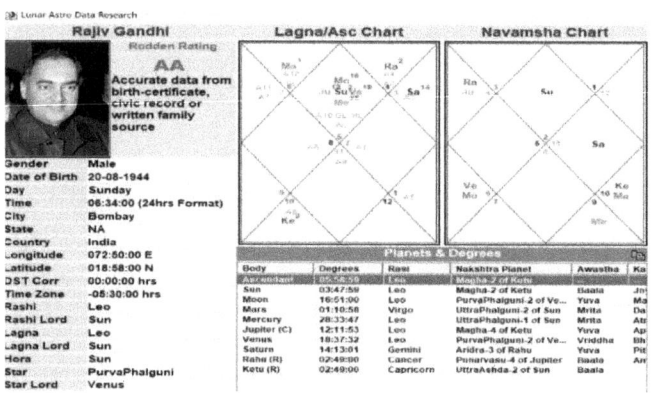

Here, in the above chart, the third house lord is Venus, being in debilitation in Navamsha. From Mars, the third house is Scorpio, and one of its lords is Ketu.

It proves the above dictum that Rajiv Gandhi became the youngest.

Ch 2

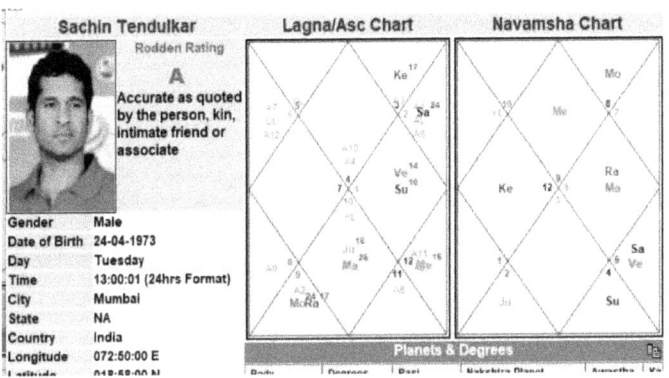

Above Chart third lord mercury debilitation. As we know Sachin Tendulkar is youngest among sibling.

Note: In jyotish Every dictum should be analysis with permutation and combination.

Ch 3

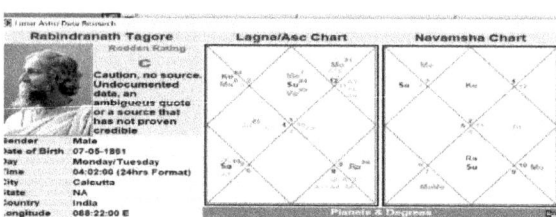

As Ketu was placed in the third house with mars. From Third from Mars is Saturn. So Rabindranath Tagore was the youngest among 13 surviving.

Ch 4

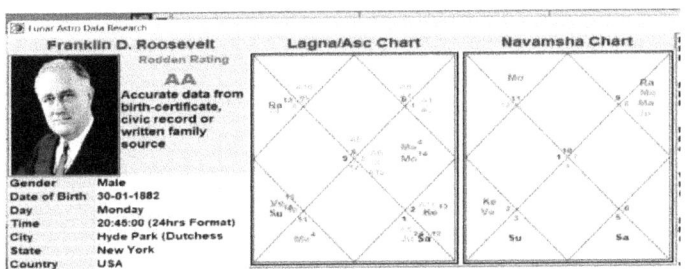

Franklin had a half-brother, James Roosevelt "Rosy" Roosevelt, from his father's previous marriage. He is the only child of his parents.

I have added these interesting charts due to curiosity Third lord is Ketu placed in exaltation house-wise but debilitation sign-wise

Rahu is one of the co-lord 11th houses of elder brothers posited in there. Rahu being a planet always gives a result like out of the box.

Rahu/Ketu being a shadowy planet never cares for social validation. One might see how beautifully it works.

As per BPHS: A male or a female co-born can be judged if the third house lord is a female planet or the third house is occupied with

Female planet the sisters were born after. Similarly, the male planet denotes male co-born. If both male and female are connected then will have both male and female co-born predicted. On the contrary, Ketu and mercury are treated as female and Saturn and Rahu are treated as male. One should judge

according to the strength of the planet and their lord.

Ch 5

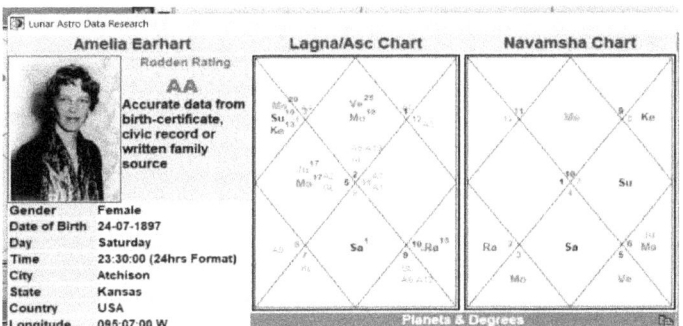

Amelia's Parents give birth to Mary Earhart in Atchison, Kansas. Two years later, Muriel, her sister, is born. Interesting objects to look at The third house lord is disposed of as follows: he is exalted. Here are some charts where the oldest sibling from the third house is placed on the planet.

To determine the oldest, one must look at the eleventh house, which includes Jupiter's Karaka, Rahu, and Lord Saturn. If these planets are associated with Karaka Mars or the third house and its ruler. The oldest among all can then be judged.

Ch 6

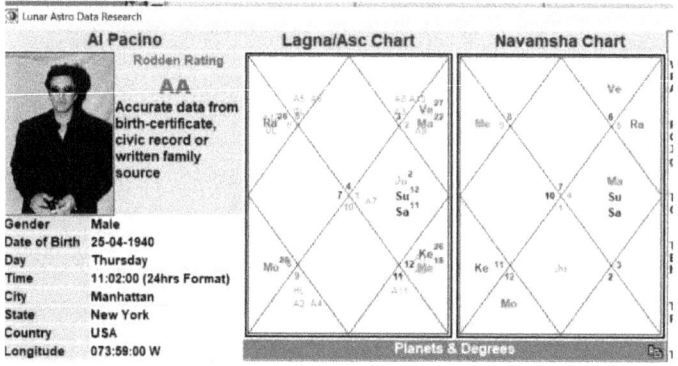

He is his parents' only child. The third house lord aspected his own house. He is positioned in exaltion Rahu.

Ch 7

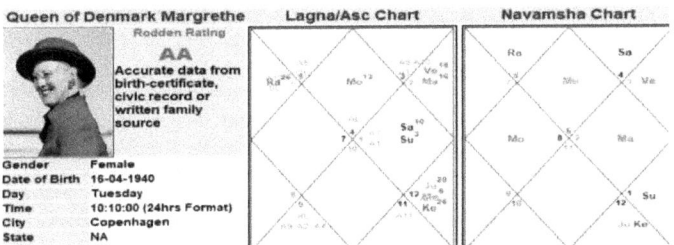

She had no brother and sister. First born to the parents.

Ch 8

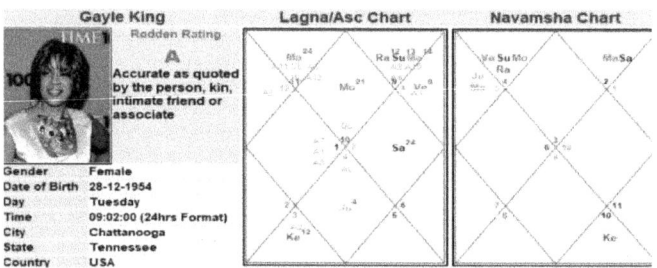

Born on December 28, 1954, Gayle King is an American television personality, writer, and broadcast journalist for CBS News. She co-hosts CBS Mornings, the network's main morning show, and CBS This Morning, its predecessor. She works for O, The Oprah Magazine, as an editor-at-large as well.

King was included in the list of the "100 Most Influential People of 2019" by Time magazine.

She is the eldest of four sisters. Here Jupiter is lord of the third {significator of the eleventh house} and is in exaltation

According to BP HS, if the third lord and Mars are together in the 8th house, it can harm siblings.

CH 9

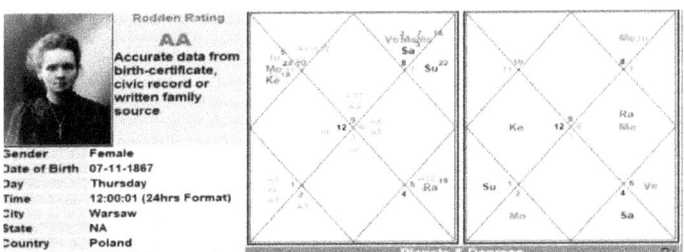

She was the youngest child. Her elder sister and mother both died from TB. Her third house lord Saturn was connected with Mars in the Scorpio sign,

which is the natural 8th house of Kaal Purush Kundali.

The classical text BPHS says: The sun in 3rd house will destroy the preborn. The afterborn will be destroyed if Saturn is placed in the third house. In the same situation, mars will destroy both preborn and later born.

Ch 10

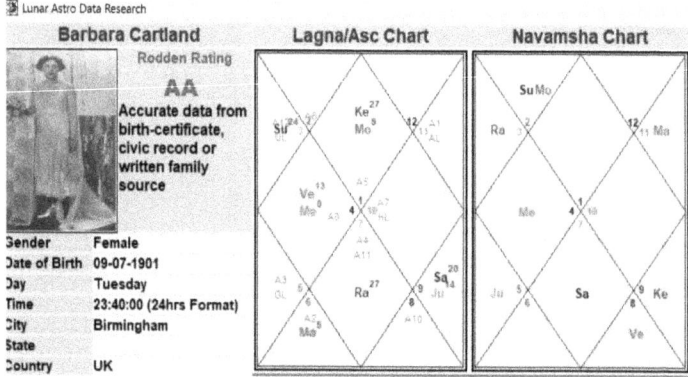

Known as the "Queen of Romance," Dame Mary Barbara Hamilton Cartland, DBE, DStJ, was an English novelist who wrote both historical and current romances, the latter of which was mostly set in the Victorian or Edwardian era. She lived from 9 July 1901 to 21 May 2000. Cartland is among the 20th century's best-selling writers globally. Cartland was born at 31 Augustus Road, Edgbaston, Birmingham.

She was the eldest child and only daughter of Major James Bertram "Bertie" Falkner Cartland[9] (1876–1918), a British Army officer, and his wife, Mary Hamilton Scobell, also known as "Polly."

The native was an only child, as we discovered when we looked at the third dwelling.

CH 11

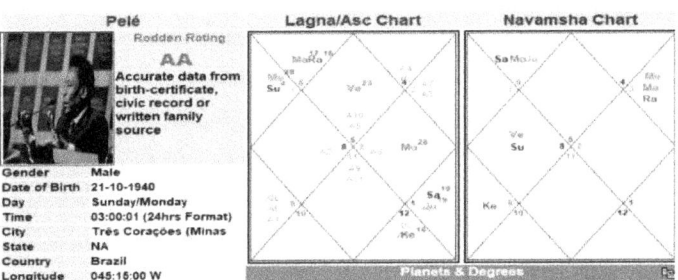

Edson Arantes do Nascimento, a Brazilian professional football player who played forward, was most popularly known by his moniker Pelé. He was one of the most prosperous and well-liked sports stars of the 20th century and is largely considered one of the greatest players of all time. He was the older of his two siblings; the younger, Zoca, was also a Santos player, though not as good. He bears the American inventor's name.

The sun and mercury are in the third house here, but the sun and Venus are in the opposite house. Despite having two younger siblings, the dictum that a native person does not have preborn siblings is still true. As I have stated, there is no one-line rule. It resembles numerous combinations and permutations.

Point of Observation

1. When the third house lord is strong and the third house from Mars is supportive, there is a promise of having

siblings, provided that Scorpio or Ketu is not connected to the third house.

2 "If Jupiter, Saturn, or Rahu are positioned in the third house, it increases the probability of the individual being the eldest among their siblings. Similarly, if Sagittarius or Aquarius is present in the third house, it also increases the likelihood of being the eldest among siblings."

3 . If the third house is occupied by a female planet and the third lord is also female, it indicates the birth of a female child, similarly, for males.

4. If Rahu is in the third house and a malefic planet influences the third lord, then the person may be an only child. Either the eldest among the genders. It is important also to consider the third from Mars.

5. A powerful Jupiter in the third house can make the eldest among genders.

CH 12

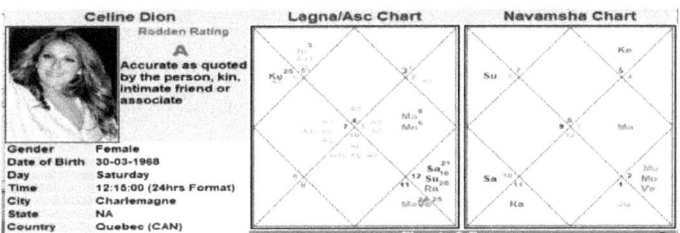

Ketu is positioned in the third house, and the third lord is in the Aquarius sign with Venus. She is the youngest among 13 siblings. Interestingly, she has more female siblings than male, which satisfies our principle.

- The third house's connection with the Sun may suggest an authoritative elder sibling, as it represents authority and fatherly figures.
- The Moon's placement in the third house may indicate a nurturing and caring relationship with siblings, representing emotions and nurturing.
- Mars' influence on the third house may suggest a potentially competitive and dynamic relationship with siblings, representing energy, aggression, and competitiveness.
- A strong Mercury in the birth chart may indicate good rapport and intellectual exchanges with siblings since it governs communication, intellect, and siblings.

- Jupiter's influence on the third house may indicate a supportive and harmonious relationship with siblings, representing wisdom, knowledge, and expansion.
- A favourable Venus in the third house may indicate a loving and harmonious relationship with siblings, characterized by shared interests and enjoyment, as Venus signifies love, harmony, and pleasures.
- Saturn's influence on the third house may suggest a more serious and burdensome relationship with siblings, possibly marked by a distance or age gap, as it represents discipline, responsibility, and hardships.
- Rahu's influence on the third house may indicate unusual or unpredictable dynamics with siblings, as well as the potential for misunderstandings or conflicts, as it represents obsession, desires, and unconventional behaviour.
- Ketu's influence on the third house may suggest a less conventional or distant relationship with siblings, marked by spiritual or philosophical connections, as it signifies detachment, spirituality, and past-life karma.
- A conjunction of Sun and Mercury in the third house may suggest a close bond with siblings based on intellectual pursuits and shared interests.
- A conjunction of Moon and Venus in the third house may indicate a deeply affectionate and emotionally supportive relationship with siblings.
- An opposition between Mars and Saturn involving the third house may indicate conflicts or power struggles

with siblings, potentially leading to rivalry or resentment.

- A harmonious trine aspect between Jupiter and Rahu involving the third house may indicate a supportive and expansive relationship with siblings, often marked by shared ideals and aspirations.

- A conjunction of Venus and Ketu in the third house may suggest unconventional or spiritually oriented connections with siblings, characterized by a sense of detachment or non-attachment.

- A square aspect between Sun and Moon involving the third house may suggest conflicts or differences in temperament with siblings, leading to emotional tension or misunderstandings.

- A sextile aspect between Mercury and Jupiter involving the third house can indicate a positive and intellectually stimulating relationship with siblings, fostering growth and mutual understanding.

- A parallel aspect between Mars and Venus involving the third house may suggest passionate and sometimes volatile interactions with siblings, marked by intense emotions and desires.

- A conjunction of Saturn and Rahu in the third house may indicate challenging dynamics with siblings, potentially involving karmic lessons or unresolved issues from the past.

- A trine aspect between Jupiter and Ketu involving the third house may suggest a spiritually inclined and philosophical relationship with siblings, marked by a sense of detachment and higher wisdom.

- A stellium involving the Sun, Mercury, and Mars in the third house can indicate a highly active and dynamic relationship with siblings, often characterized by intense communication, competitiveness, and drive for success.

Power of inner potentiality

This remarkable house possesses an intriguing duality - it has both the power to create and destroy. It belongs to Mahesh, a name that is synonymous with samhara, which is known as the destroyer of one's misery. As per Hindu astrology, the Brahma-Vishnu-Mahesh concept is related to the Zodiac cycle. According to this concept, the first house represents Brahma, the creator of the universe, the second house represents Vishnu, the preserver of the universe, and the third house represents Maheswara, the destroyer of all that exists. Thus, this house, which is associated with Mahesh, is believed to be capable of unleashing intense and transformative energies that are capable of both creating and destroying one's life.

This particular house demands a consistent repetition of one's daily activities to maintain order and function properly. The key to achieving our goals is through relentless effort and persistence, consistently repeating the same actions until we reach our desired outcome. Consistency in our actions is the key to unlocking success.

This house places great importance on both imagination and intelligence. It is believed that combining these two qualities is essential for success in any endeavour. In addition, this house is also associated with the initiation mantra chanting, a ritualistic process that involves the repetition of specific sounds or words. It is said that this practice can bring about a sense of calm and clarity, helping individuals to focus their minds and achieve their goals. Overall, this house is a place of innovation, creativity, and spiritual growth.

There is a well-known temple called Chakrshwara Mahadev Mandir in Nalasopara, Mumbai. Inside the temple, you can find an ancient statue of Vishwakarma that is believed to be around 1000 years old. What's fascinating about the statue is that it has an instrument that looks like a theodolite in the upper right hand. It seems as if someone is peering through it to take measurements. A theodolite is an optical instrument that is used for measuring angles between visible points in both the horizontal and vertical planes. Hindu mythology is replete with fascinating stories and characters, and one such character is Vishwakarma. Known as the divine architect and craftsman of the gods, Vishwakarma is a figure of immense significance in Hinduism. According to legend, Vishwakarma was entrusted with the mammoth task of constructing Hastinapur, the capital of the Kuru kingdom. Hastinapur was not merely a city, but a symbol of power, prestige, and prosperity. It was the birthplace of the Pandavas and Kauravas, two of the most well-known and celebrated figures in Hindu mythology. Vishwakarma's skill, expertise, and dedication were instrumental in bringing Hastinapur to life, and his legacy continues to inspire awe and admiration to this day.

According to Hindu mythology, Vishwakarma was an incredibly skilled and talented architect and engineer. He was known for his unmatched craftsmanship and meticulous attention to detail. Legend has it that he was the one who designed and built Hastinapur, a magnificent city that was considered to be worthy of the gods themselves.

Using his expertise in architecture and engineering, Vishwakarma created grand palaces that were adorned with intricate carvings and designs. He also built intricate temples that were a testament to his artistic prowess and engineering skills. The city was fortified with walls that were both strong and beautiful, and every structure was built to perfection.

In short, Vishwakarma's contribution to the city of Hastinapur was nothing short of extraordinary. His work remains a testament to his unparalleled talent and skill and, to this day, is considered to be one of the most impressive feats of engineering and architecture in Hindu mythology.

The significator of the Third house Mars

The third house significator is Mars. Mars is known as the planet of Angaraka, and it provides an abundant supply of fuel to the body. It is considered the true warrior among all living organisms, and it gives energy to all creatures on Earth. Without it, living organisms might not exist, and it is essential for the survival of all creatures. It is also known as the controller of passion and anger, and it is referred to by many names such as Mars, Bhauma, Bhumiputra, Angarika, Kuja, Mangala, and more.

In the realm of sports, Mars and the ruler of the Third House are believed to have significant influence. Achieving success in any field requires sustained and persistent efforts instead of sporadic bursts of energy.

Points of observation :

Participating in sports that require physical strength and stamina is crucial to excelling in activities such as running, sky diving, jumping, racing, cricket, soccer, football, swimming, and scuba diving. The third house lord and Mars play vital roles in determining one's success in these sports.

Ch 1

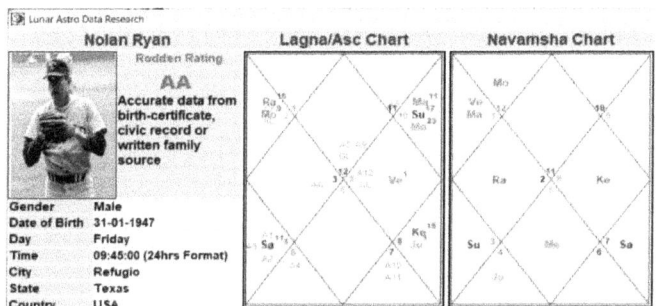

Observation: Rahu in the third house makes one hungry but never satisfied and makes one keep working hard. The exalted moon is present in the third house, and Mars is also in exaltation. The lord of the third house is in the tenth house of Sagittarius. A good Mars makes one physically fit. The third house lord is in the tenth house, making one an achiever in life.

Lynn Nolan Ryan Jr. was an American professional baseball pitcher and sports executive, nicknamed "the Ryan Express". He played for four different teams, namely New York Mets, California Angels, Houston Astros, and Texas Rangers, during his record 27-year career in Major League Baseball (MLB). After his retirement in 1993, he served as the chief executive officer (CEO) of the Texas Rangers and an executive advisor to the Houston Astros. In 1999, he was inducted into the Baseball Hall of Fame and is widely regarded as one of the greatest MLB pitchers of all time. Ryan was a right-handed pitcher who consistently threw pitches that were clocked above 100 miles per hour (161 km/h) and maintained this velocity throughout his career. He was also known for his devastating 12-6 curveball, which he threw at exceptional velocity for a breaking ball.

Ryan holds the record for the most no-hitters in baseball history, with seven, which is three more than any other pitcher. He is tied with Bob Feller for the most one-hitters, with 12. Ryan has also pitched 18 two-hitters. However, despite his impressive record, he never pitched a perfect game, nor did he ever win a Cy Young Award. His high walk rate was largely responsible for this. Ryan is one of only 31 players in baseball history who have played in MLB games in four different decades.

Ch 2

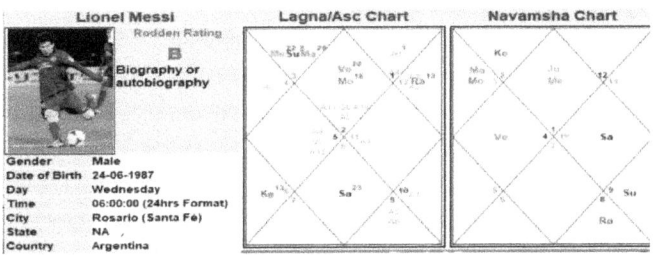

Messi is widely considered as one of the greatest football players of all time, having won eight Ballon d'Or awards, more than any other player. His playing style and skills have been compared to those of the legendary Argentine footballer, Diego Maradona. Messi is often compared to his rival, the Portuguese footballer Cristiano Ronaldo. In 2009, he was ranked second in the "World Player of the Decade 2000s" list, behind Ronaldinho but ahead of Cristiano Ronaldo. Messi has played alongside many other football greats, including Ronaldinho, Deco, Samuel Eto'o, Luis Suárez, Xavi, Andrés Iniesta, Sergio Busquets, and Neymar.

Observation :

It has been observed that the third house lord is exalted and is in conjunction with the Ascendant lord, who is positioned in the first house. Mars is present in the second house with the Sun and Mercury. Mars is also the lord of the twelfth house, which represents feet. Upon deeper analysis, it is evident that most of the energy resides in the feet.

Additionally, Rahu's aspect on the twelfth house increases the energy by ten folds, making one highly skilled. This unique combination creates a world-famous football player.

Ch 3

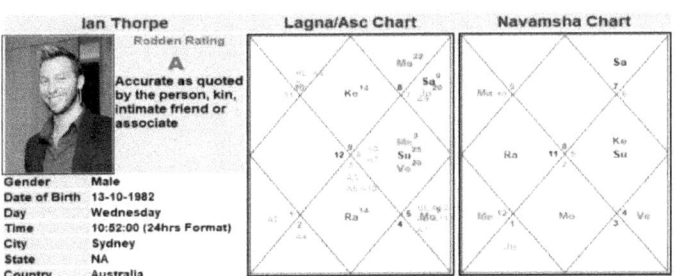

Ian Thorpe
Rodden Rating
A
Accurate as quoted by the person, kin, intimate friend or associate

Gender	Male
Date of Birth	13-10-1982
Day	Wednesday
Time	10:52:00 (24hrs Format)
City	Sydney
State	NA
Country	Australia

Ian James Thorpe AM, born on October 13, 1982, is a retired Australian swimmer. He specialized in freestyle but also competed in backstroke and individual medley. Thorpe has won five Olympic gold medals, which is the highest number of gold medals won by any Australian athlete, along with fellow swimmer Emma McKeon. At the 2000 Summer Olympics held in his hometown of Sydney, Thorpe was the most successful athlete, having won three gold and two silver medals.

Ian Thorpe, a former Australian swimmer, has achieved great success in his career. He has won a total of eleven gold medals in World Championships, which is the fifth-highest number of gold medals won by any male swimmer. Thorpe was the first person to be named Swimming World Swimmer of the Year four times, and he was also the Australian Swimmer of the Year from 1999 to 2003. Because of his outstanding athletic achievements, he was considered one of Australia's most popular athletes. In

2000, he was recognised as the Young Australian of the Year.

Observation

Here, the Third house, both the lord in exaltation. And Mars is in his sign. But exaltation in navamsa. Navamsha which shows the real dignity of the planet majorly. The third lord in the eleventh house, with the ascendent lord Jupiter, makes a successful.

Ch 4

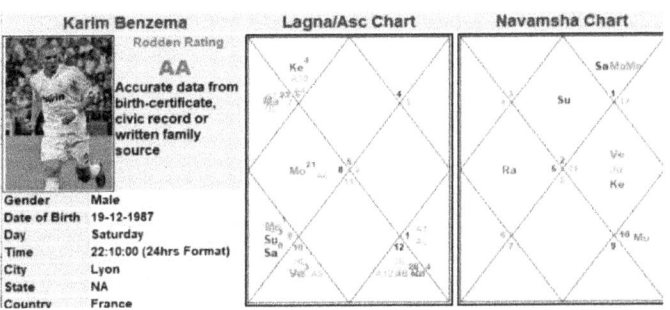

French football player Karim Mostafa Benzema captains and plays as a striker for Al-Ittihad in the Saudi Pro League. One of the greatest strikers of all time, Karim Benzema is a creative forward recognized for his technical prowess, field vision, and adaptability. He is Real Madrid's second-highest goalscorer and leading assist producer of all time. With Real Madrid, he took home 24 trophies, including five UEFA Champions League wins, three Copa del Reys, and four La Liga crowns.

Observation

Here, the significator Mars is in the third house in the Libra sign, which shows excellent physical ability and drives towards sports. In other aspects, the 9th house lord aspecting his own house gives rise to fortune in sports.

Ch 5

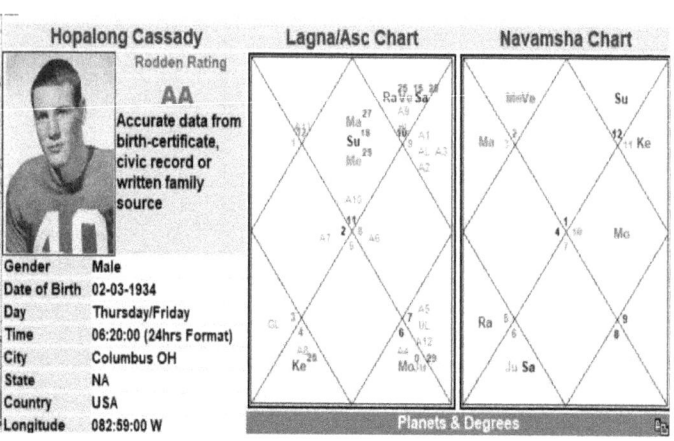

American football halfback and split end Howard Albert "Hopalong" Cassady (March 2, 1934 – September 20, 2019) was a member of the National Football League (NFL). He was a member of the Ohio State Buckeyes football team, where he was the 1955 Heisman Trophy winner. During his eight seasons in the NFL, Cassady spent seven of them as a player with the Detroit Lions, with whom he shared the 1957 NFL Championship Game. In 1979, he was admitted to the College Football Hall of Fame.

In the above chart, the significator is the third house lord placed in the first house of astrology, making him a champion in football. Mars, being lord of both 10th and third posited in the ascendant (house of self-effort and fame), makes another level of victory.

One of the most well-known Indian myths, the story of Eklavya, from the Hindu epic Mahabharata, illustrates many kinds of abilities and proficiencies.

A young prince from the Nishad clan was named Eklavya. His passion was archery, and he had an unwavering respect for the legendary archery expert Dron Acharya. The Pandavas and Kauravas were among the Kuru princes who learned archery from Dron Acharya, the royal instructor, who had vowed to instruct only members of the royal family and those of higher status.

Eklavya was unfazed by this limitation and decided to learn archery. He made a statue of Dron Acharya and dedicated his practice to it, considering it to be his master. By sheer willpower, Eklavya achieved mastery over The Pandavas and came upon Eklavya in the forest one day while they were hunting. Inspired by his skill, they asked to see his guru. Even though Eklavya never took formal tuition from Dronacharya, he demonstrated his devotion to him.

When Dron Acharya learned about it, he chose to put Eklavya's extraordinary talent to the test because he felt threatened. To make the customary offering of a pupil to their master, known as "guru dakshina," Dronacharya went up to Eklavya and asked for his right thumb. Encumbered by his honor code, Eklavya did not hesitate to cut off his thumb and give it to Dronacharya, so he could no longer shoot arrows with the same accuracy.

The story of Eklavya showcases a variety of admirable qualities such as dedication, perseverance, ability, and talent. Eklavya's unwavering commitment and efforts enabled him to master the art of archery on his own. He did not receive any formal training from a master, but his natural aptitude for archery helped him become a skilled archer. Eklavya displayed flexibility and resourcefulness to overcome various obstacles and achieve his goals.

Ch 6

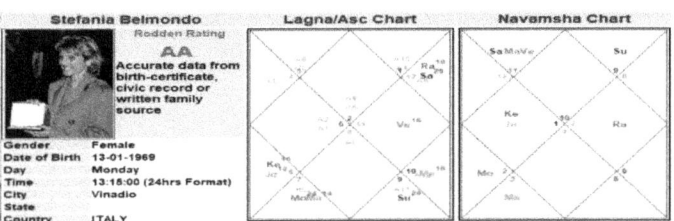

Stefania Belmondo (born 13 January 1969) is an Italian former cross-country skier, a two-time Olympic champion and a four-time world champion in her career.

In the above chart, the third lord moon got exaltation in Navimsha, and the disposition of the moon, Venus, is with Saturn, and Mars makes a high flyer.

Ch 7

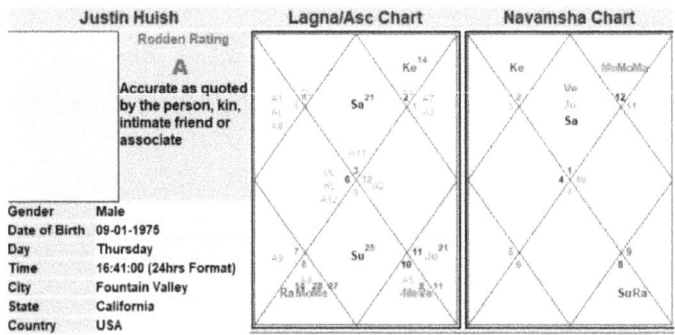

Justin Grant Huish was an American archer who won two gold medals in the 1996 Atlanta Olympics. Despite being an unorthodox character known for his wrap-around shades, backward baseball cap, ponytail and earring, Huish captivated the crowd with his impressive victories in the individual and team events. In the individual event, Huish was ranked no higher than 24th in the world at the time, but he rose to the occasion and defeated Sweden's Magnus Pettersson 112-107 in the final. Huish became the first male archer to win two Olympic gold medals, which helped increase the sport's popularity. South Korea's Ku Bon-chan later matched his feat at the 2016 Summer Olympics. Huish was also credited with encouraging actress Geena Davis to take up archery.

When Justin Huish was in ninth grade, he was interested in skateboarding and lived on a street called Broken Arrow. At the time, he thought archery was not very interesting.

However, when his parents opened Arrowsmith Archery, he became interested in working there. He started practising archery at the age of 14, and he would stand in the middle of the street and shoot arrows through the front door of his garage, through the back door of his garage, and into a target in his backyard. Amazingly, only three years after starting archery, Justin Huish won the intermediate age division at the National Archery Association's Outdoor Target Championships. He went on to win significant victories at the 1993 US Collegiate Championships and the 1995 US Target Championships. Despite only joining the US National Team in 1994, Justin Huish quickly established himself as a top archer.

Observation

The third lord, the sun, is placed in the 7th house, Sagittarius. The Sagittarius sign plays a key role in archery. The disposition of the sun placed in the 9th house aspecting the third house makes one succeed.

Ch 8

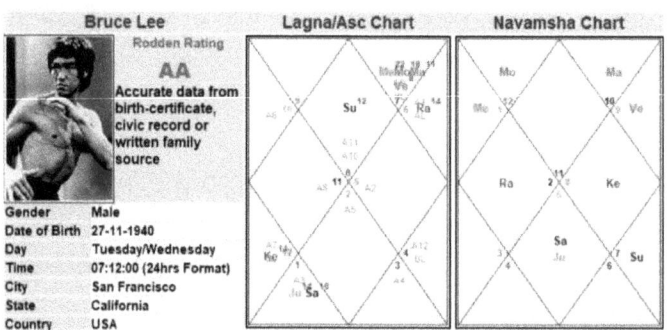

"I fear not the man who has practiced 10,000 kicks once, but I fear the man who has practiced one kick 10,000 times."

Bruce Lee was a Hong Kong-American martial artist and actor and founder of Jeet Kune Do. He is considered one of the most influential martial artists of all time, credited with promoting Hong Kong action cinema and changing the way Chinese people were presented in American films. Lee was known for his exceptional physical fitness and strength, which he achieved through a dedicated fitness regimen. However, after his match with Wong Jack-man in 1965, Lee changed his approach to martial arts training. He believed that many martial artists didn't devote enough time to physical conditioning, so he included all aspects of total fitness in his training, such as muscular strength, muscular endurance, cardiovascular endurance, and flexibility. Lee used traditional bodybuilding techniques to build muscle mass but not to an extent that could decrease his speed or flexibility. He believed that mental and spiritual preparation was just as important as physical training to achieve success in martial arts skills.

Mars and Capricorn played key roles in martial arts skills. This is evident from Saturn's disposition with Jupiter (the planet of expansion) in exaltation in Navmsha.

Ch 9

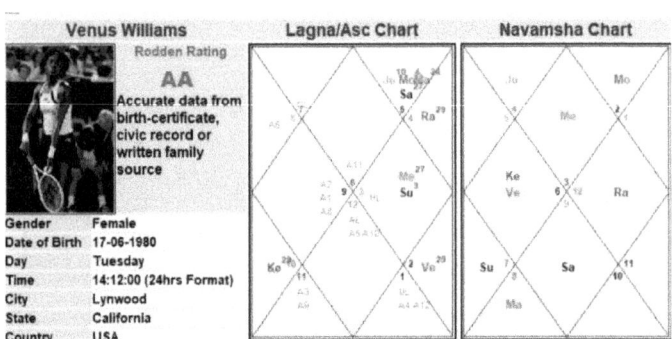

Venus Williams
Rodden Rating
AA
Accurate data from birth-certificate, civic record or written family source

Gender	Female
Date of Birth	17-06-1980
Day	Tuesday
Time	14:12:00 (24hrs Format)
City	Lynwood
State	California
Country	USA

Venus Ebony Starr Williams is a professional tennis player from the United States. She has been ranked as the world's No. 1 player in both singles and doubles. Williams has won seven Grand Slam singles titles, five at Wimbledon and two at the US Open. She is widely considered to be one of the greatest tennis players of all time due to her impressive skills and accomplishments. Williams is an aggressive player with an all-court game, which leads to her accumulating large numbers of both winners and unforced errors. She has powerful groundstrokes on both sides and is capable of hitting her forehand and backhand flat, and with topspin. Williams is also skilled at hitting her backhand with slices to slow down rallies and disrupt the pace within rallies. Her serve is powerful, which allows her to serve numerous aces in any match.

The third house aspected by the benefic planet and ascendant lord is in the tenth house with the sun making budhaaditya Raj yog.

Ch 10

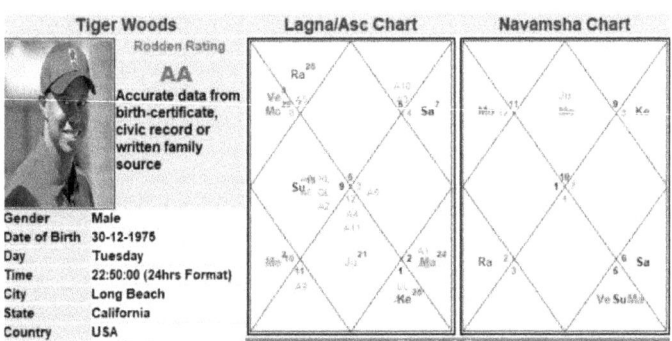

Eldrick Tont "Tiger" Woods is an accomplished American professional golfer. He is currently tied for first place in PGA Tour wins, ranks second in men's major championships, and holds numerous golf records. Woods is considered one of the greatest golfers of all time and one of the most famous athletes in modern history. He has been inducted into the esteemed World Golf Hall of Fame.

Usually, Venus and the debilitated moon in the third house makes one entitlement self-deprivation, and hard work, but risk taker Mars aspecting own house, empowering the house. Mars is placed in the 9th house as the third lord and there is an exchange between the lords of the 9th and 3rd houses.

Singer Astrology

The story of Brahma-Viraj and Vach-Viraj originates from Hindu mythology, particularly from the Puranas. It narrates the celestial union of Brahma, the creator god, with his daughter Vach, who represents speech and knowledge. According to the myth, Brahma desired to create the universe and all its beings. To accomplish this monumental task, he needed a consort who possessed the power of speech and wisdom. Brahma realised that Vach, his daughter, embodied these qualities and thus approached her for union. Initially, Vach was hesitant and reluctant to marry her own father. She expressed her concerns and questioned the moral implications of such a union. However, Brahma assured her that their relationship transcended the earthly norms and was essential for the creation and sustenance of the universe.

Convinced by Brahma's explanation and recognising her duty, Vach agreed to marry him. Their union symbolised the fusion of creative energy (Brahma) with the power of speech and knowledge (Vach), which were necessary for the manifestation and evolution of the cosmos.

Together, Brahma and Vach embarked on the divine task of creation. With his creative prowess, Brahma shaped the physical forms of the universe, while Vach infused them with intelligence, wisdom, and the ability to communicate. Their union brought forth the creation of the Vedas, the sacred scriptures of Hinduism, which are believed to embody cosmic knowledge and eternal truths. Vach, also known as Saraswati, became revered as the goddess of speech, learning, and the arts.

Benfica Panet connection with Third house

Moon, Venus and Mercury play a crucial connection with the third house and its lord to be a singer.

In Vedic astrology, the 2nd, 3rd, or 5th house are believed to influence a person's singing ability significantly. This is because these houses are associated with important factors such as communication, speech, creativity, and artistic expression, which are all fundamental components of singing. For instance, the 2nd house is linked to the person's voice and how it sounds, while the 3rd house is associated with the style and flow of communication. The 5th house, the other house is related to creative self-expression, including music and singing.

Moreover, placing specific planets in these houses can further impact a person's musical talents. For example, Venus is known as the planet of love, beauty, and harmony, and its placement in any of these houses can enhance one's singing ability. Mercury, the planet of communication and intelligence, can also contribute to people's ability to express themselves through singing. Finally, the Moon is associated with emotions, creativity, and imagination, which are all crucial elements in singing. Therefore, placing these planets in the 2nd, 3rd, or 5th house can provide an added advantage to anyone who wants to excel in singing.

Venus holds significant influence: In Vedic astrology, Venus is known as the planet of creativity, arts, and aesthetics. A strong and well-placed Venus in the natal chart may indicate the presence of musical talent. When Venus is in conjunction with or aspecting the Moon or Mercury, it can further enhance one's musical abilities. In Kalpurush Kundali, Taurus is the 2nd lord where the moon gets exalted. Moon and Venus are artistic planets. Mercury is the way one generates sounds or audibles.

Singing voices can be associated with different planets. This belief stems from the idea that celestial bodies influence artistic expression.

1. Sun: A singing voice influenced by the Sun can be powerful, commanding, and full of vitality. It may have a warm, resonant quality that captures audiences' attention. Like Patriarchy songs. Opera singers perform in operas with powerful voices and orchestral accompaniment in large theatres after receiving training in classical music.

2. Moon: A singing voice influenced by the Moon can be emotionally expressive, with a wide range of moods and tones. It can also be soothing and nurturing, evoking deep feelings and connections in listeners. Gospel singers express their deep faith and conviction through spiritual and religious music. They may perform in churches, choirs, or as solo artists, using a soulful and emotive style. Immensely emotional songs.

3. Mercury: Mercury rules communication and expression, so a singing voice influenced by Mercury may be versatile, agile, and articulate. It could excel in delivering complex lyrics with precision and clarity. Classical crossover singers combine classical techniques with popular music styles, showcasing their versatility and operatic training to a wider audience.   Playful songs

4. Venus: Venus is associated with beauty and harmony, so a singing voice influenced by Venus might be melodious, sweet, and pleasing to the ear. It may possess a natural charm and grace that captivates listeners. Jazz singers are highly skilled in improvisation, interpretation, and scat singing. They possess a soulful voice and a great sense of rhythm, often performing standards.

5. Mars: A singing voice influenced by Mars might convey energy, passion, and intensity, driving forward with determination and vigour. Pop singers typically perform popular music genres such as pop, rock, R&B, and dance. They often have a wide vocal range and a charismatic stage presence. Rock singers lead rock bands, delivering powerful vocals over electric guitar-driven music. Their voices may be gritty or smooth, depending on the subgenre of rock.

6. Saturn: Saturn is associated with discipline and structure. A Saturnian singing voice might be precise, controlled, and disciplined. It could excel in classical or technical styles, with a focus on technique and mastery. Country singers specialize in country music, featuring storytelling lyrics, twangy vocals, and elements of folk and blues. They often sing about themes like love, heartbreak, and rural life. Folk singers perform traditional or contemporary folk music, often accompanied by acoustic instruments like guitar or banjo. They focus on storytelling and cultural heritage in their songs.

7. Jupiter: Jupiter is associated with growth so that a Jupiter-influenced singing voice may be grand, expansive, and larger than life. It could have a rich, operatic quality

capable of filling vast spaces with its resonance. Indie singer-songwriters blend folk, rock, and alternative music to create authentic, introspective songs.

Ch 11

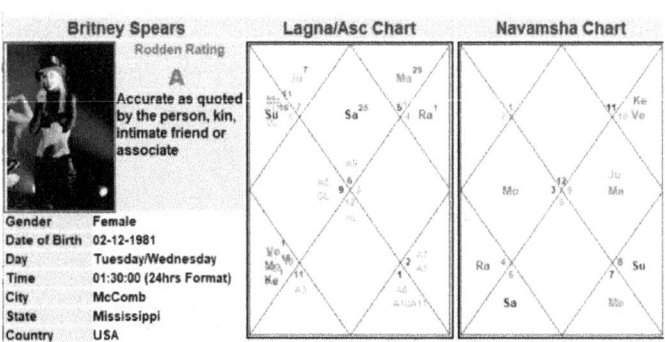

Britney Jean Spears, an American singer, was born on December 2, 1981. She is famously known as the "Princess of Pop" and is credited with revitalizing teen pop during the late 1990s and early 2000s. She has sold over 150 million records globally and is considered one of the world's best-selling music artists. Her contributions to the music industry have earned her numerous awards and accolades, including a Grammy Award, six MTV Video Music Awards, seven Billboard Music Awards (including the Millennium Award), the inaugural Radio Disney Icon Award, and a star on the Hollywood Walk of Fame. Furthermore, she was awarded the Michael Jackson Video Vanguard Award for her highly choreographed videos.

There is an exchange between the third lord and the twelfth lord posited with the ascendant, and the tenth lord mercury gives significance rise.

Ch 12

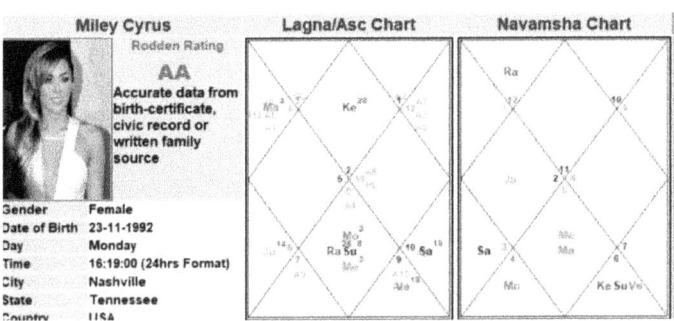

Miley Ray Cyrus was born on November 23, 1992, under the name Destiny Hope Cyrus. She is an actress, singer, and songwriter who has gained fame as a pop icon for her evolving style and artistry. In the 2000s era, she was known as the "Teen Queen," and she is one of the few child stars who's had a successful music career as an adult. Billy Ray Cyrus, a country singer, is her father, and she became a teen idol at the age of 13 when she played the lead character in the Disney Channel's television series Hannah Montana between 2006 and 2011. As Hannah Montana, she notched up two number-one soundtracks and a US top-ten single, making her a success on the Billboard charts.

Mars is in the third house disposition with the lord of the 10th house, Rahu, in the seventh house. Mars, associated with mercury in Naivasha, makes one unique voice in her singing ability.

Ch 13

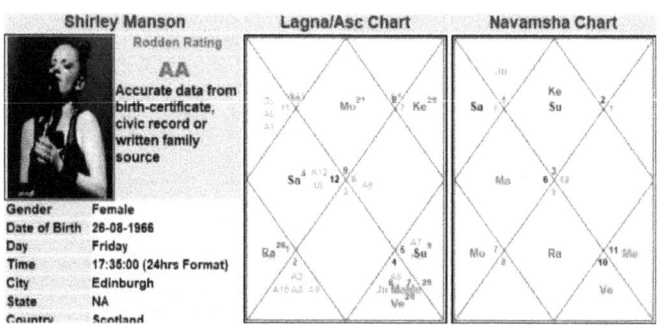

Shirley Ann Manson FRSA, born on August 26, 1966, is a Scottish musician and actress. She is well-known for being the lead singer of the alternative rock band Garbage, as well as the host of The Jump with Shirley Manson (2019-2021). Manson is known for her direct style, rebellious attitude, and unique deep voice. Throughout her career, she has travelled between her hometown of Edinburgh and the United States to record with Garbage, which was originally formed in Madison, Wisconsin. She resides and works mostly in Los Angeles while maintaining a secondary residence in Edinburgh.

Ch 14

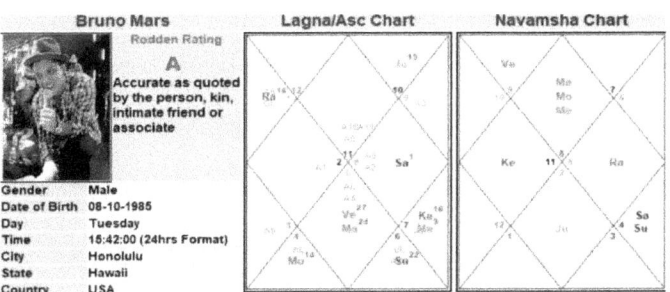

Gender Male
Date of Birth 08-10-1985
Day Tuesday
Time 16:42:00 (24hrs Format)
City Honolulu
State Hawaii
Country USA

Peter Gene Hernandez, born on October 8, 1985, is a well-known American singer-songwriter professionally known as Bruno Mars. He is known for his remarkable stage performances, retro showmanship, and versatility in a wide range of musical genres such as pop, R&B, funk, soul, reggae, disco, and rock. Mars performs with his band, The Hooligans, who play a variety of instruments including electric guitar, bass, piano, keyboards, drums, and horns, and also serve as backup singers and disco dancers. In 2021, he joined forces with Anderson. Paak to form Silk Sonic, the American musical super duo.

Scientist

Analytical aspects are an important factor in determining an individual's scientific study and research approach. The favourable placement of Mercury and Saturn in a birth chart suggests that the person is methodical and disciplined. However, if there are aspects between Mercury and Pluto, it might indicate that the person has a strong curiosity and a drive to reveal hidden truths.

Uranus is associated with sudden insights, innovation, and invention. If Uranus is significantly placed in a person's birth chart, such as in angular houses (1st, 4th, 7th, or 10th) or making significant aspects to personal planets like Sun, Moon, Mercury, Venus, or Mars, it could indicate a natural talent for inventive thinking.

Mercury governs intellect, communication, and the thought process. Uranus represents innovation. When there is a strong aspect (conjunction, sextile, trine) between Mercury and Uranus, it suggests that the person has a quick, inventive mind that is capable of thinking outside the box.

Aquarius is a zodiac sign that is ruled by Uranus and is often associated with originality, invention, and unconventional thinking. If someone has a strong emphasis on Aquarius placements in their birth chart, such as the Sun, Moon, Ascendant, or multiple planets in Aquarius, it can suggest that they have an innovative and visionary personality.

The third house is associated with communication, learning, and intellectual pursuits, while the eleventh house symbolises originality, innovation, and social networks. Mercury, Uranus, or their rulers are placed in these houses, which can indicate a talent for inventiveness and the ability to disseminate ideas.

In a picturesque village, nestled amidst rolling hills, where the whispering winds carried tales of the past and the rustling leaves sang melodies of ancient times, there stood a humble radio station known as Akashvani. Secluded from the bustling world, it served as a means of connection, broadcasting stories, news, and music to the far corners of the land.

At the core of Akashvani was Gaurishankar, an experienced broadcaster with a soothing voice that echoed like a gentle summer breeze. Each morning, he would ascend the wooden stairs of the station, decorated with creeping ivy, to reach the studio located atop the hill. He would work his magic there, surrounded by vintage equipment and crackling vinyl records, bringing the airwaves to life.

The people of the village depended on Akashvani for more than just the latest news and entertainment. It was their only connection to the outside world. From reports of wars happening in far-off places to the calming tunes of classical ragas, Akashvani was their portal to the universe beyond their small community.

As the sun set behind the horizon, casting an amber glow over the village, a fierce storm suddenly descended upon the land. Thunder roared like an angry deity and lightning danced across the darkened sky. The radio station, perched atop the hill, trembled under the onslaught of nature's fury.

Despite the strong wind and thunder outside, Gaurishankar was working inside the studio with great focus and determination. However, as luck would have it, a bolt of lightning hit the old transmitter, causing sparks to fly and plunging Akashvani into darkness.

The villagers were devastated when Akashvani went missing, their hearts filled with worry and longing for days. The silence that enveloped their community made everything seem dull and dreary. However, amidst their despair, a glimmer of hope appeared like a beam of light in the darkness, offering a ray of optimism to those who needed it most.

The villagers were determined to bring back Akashvani to its former glory. They rallied together with unyielding spirits, just like the roots of the ancient banyan tree. With axes, saws, hammers and nails, they worked tirelessly day and night, rebuilding the shattered transmitter and rejuvenating the weather-beaten station.

One morning, when the sun was shining and creating a beautiful golden hue on the hills, Akashvani suddenly came back to life. The static noise was heard, the speakers hummed, and the voice of Gaurishankar echoed once again across the land. From that day on, Akashvani flourished more than ever before, and its reach extended far beyond the village boundaries. It became a symbol of resilience and a testament to the unbreakable spirit of the community.

Akashvani's echoes reverberated for years, weaving tales of hope and perseverance. It remained etched in the hearts of listeners, a beacon of light and a melody that soared above life's storms.

Ch 15

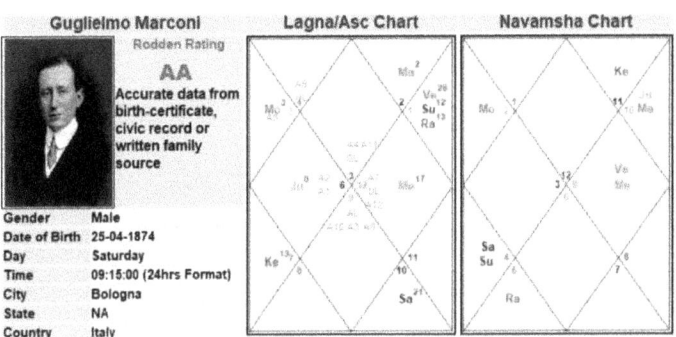

Guglielmo Giovanni Maria Marconi was a renowned Italian inventor and electrical engineer born on April 25th, 1874. He is famous for his creation of an effective wireless telegraph system based on radio waves. This invention led to Marconi being recognized as the inventor of radio. In 1909, he shared the Nobel Prize in Physics with Karl Ferdinand Braun, in appreciation of their contribution to the development of wireless telegraphy. Apart from his inventions, Marconi was also a successful entrepreneur and the founder of The Wireless Telegraph & Signal Company in the United Kingdom in 1897. This company later became known as the Marconi Company. In 1929, King Victor Emmanuel III of Italy ennobled Marconi as a Marchese (marquis), and in 1931, he established Vatican Radio for Pope Pius XI.

The exalted third lord in the 11th house makes one most successful in all endeavours, while Rahu and Venu give ideas that are out of the box.

Ch 16

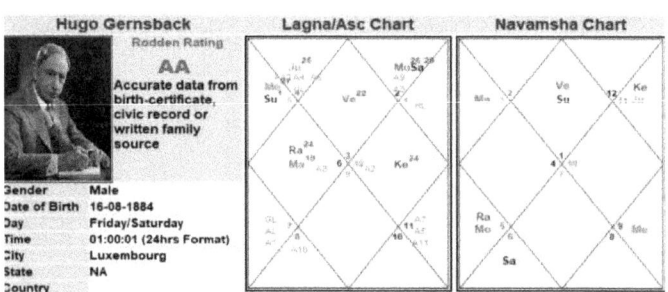

Gender	Male
Date of Birth	16-08-1884
Day	Friday/Saturday
Time	01:00:01 (24hrs Format)
City	Luxembourg
State	NA
Country	

Hugo Gernsback, born as Hugo Gernsbacher on August 16, 1884, was a magazine publisher and editor from America. He is widely known for being the publisher of the first science fiction magazine, Amazing Stories. Gernsback's contribution to the genre as a publisher was so significant that he is often called "The Father of Science Fiction", along with Jules Verne and H. G. Wells. In his honour, the annual awards presented at the World Science Fiction Convention are named the "Hugos".

Gernsback held 80 patents until his death in New York City on August 19, 1967. His first patent was a new method for manufacturing dry cell batteries, which he applied for on June 28, 1906, and was granted on February 5, 1907. Among his many inventions are a combined electric hair brush and comb, which he patented in 1912 (U.S. patent 1,016,138), an ear cushion patented in 1927 (U.S. patent 1,514,152), and a hydraulic fishery patented in 1955 (U.S. patent 2,718,083). Gernsback wrote a work called Music for the Deaf in The

Electrical Experimenter, in which he described the Physio phone. The Physio phone was a device that could convert audio into electrical impulses that could be detected by humans. Gernsback advocated for this device as a method of allowing the deaf to experience music.

Gernsback has several other patents related to Incandescent Lamp, Electro rheostat Regulators, Electro Adjustable Condenser, Detectorium, Relay, Potentiometer, Electrolytic Interrupter, Rotary Variable Condenser, Luminous Electric Mirror, Transmitter, Postal Card, Telephone Headband, Electromagnetic Sounding Device, Submersible Amusement Device, The Isolator, Apparatus for Landing Flying Machines, Tuned Telephone Receiver, Electric Valve, Detector, Acoustic Apparatus, Electrically Operated Fountain, Cord Terminal, Coil Mounting, Radio Horn, Variable Condenser, Switch, Telephone Receiver, Crystal Detector, Process for Mounting Inductances, and Depilator, Code Learner's Instrument.

The most eminent publisher has strong third houses and are connected with mercury.

Ch 17

Marie Curie

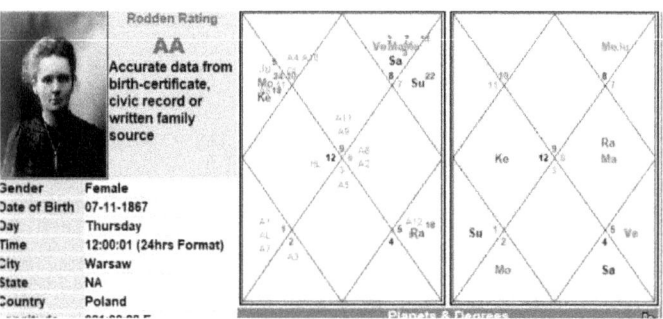

Gender: Female
Date of Birth: 07-11-1867
Day: Thursday
Time: 12:00:01 (24hrs Format)
City: Warsaw
State: NA
Country: Poland

Marie Curie, a distinguished scientist, is known for her exceptional achievements in discovering two radioactive elements, radium and polonium. Her groundbreaking research in this field has had a profound impact on modern medicine, particularly in the development of treatments for cancer. Her legacy has inspired our charity's mission to drive fundamental change in end-of-life care, with the aim of providing everyone with the opportunity to live their lives to the fullest, even in their final moments.

Jupiter's moon and Ketu in the third house, aspected by the dispositor Rahu, gave her a hunger for research. Rahu represents radioactive rays. She finally invented the X-Ray.

Ch 18

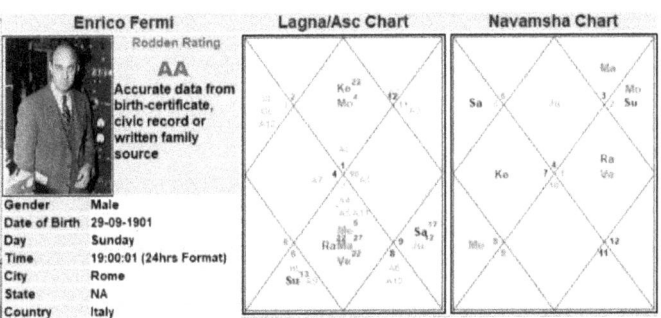

Gender	Male
Date of Birth	29-09-1901
Day	Sunday
Time	19:00:01 (24hrs Format)
City	Rome
State	NA
Country	Italy

Enrico Fermi was a renowned Italian physicist who made remarkable contributions to the fields of nuclear and theoretical physics. He was born on September 29, 1901, in Rome, Italy, and showed exceptional mathematical abilities from a young age. Fermi earned his doctorate in physics from the University of Pisa in 1922, where he studied under the esteemed Italian physicist and Nobel laureate, Orso Mario Corbino.

Fermi's early research focused on statistical mechanics, quantum theory, and the study of atomic and molecular phenomena. His work on the Fermi-Dirac statistics, which describe the behaviour of particles that obey the Pauli exclusion principle, such as electrons in a solid, gained him international recognition.

In 1938, Fermi was awarded the Nobel Prize in Physics for his work on induced radioactivity, which laid the foundation for the discovery of nuclear fission. He successfully bombarded uranium with neutrons, resulting in the creation of new radioactive elements. This groundbreaking experiment paved the way for the development of nuclear reactors and atomic bombs.

For any invention, the eighth house and its lord should be connected with the third house and its lord. In the above chart, Rahu, Me,ve, and Mars are in the seventh house.

Artist

Qi Baishi is a celebrated Chinese painter who overcame many obstacles to become one of the most famous artists of his time. Born into a family struggling with poverty, he could not afford a formal education, but he had a natural talent for painting. Despite facing numerous challenges throughout his life, including political instability, personal tragedies, and financial difficulties, he remained steadfast in his dedication to his art.

Qi Baishi's unique style was characterised by bold brushwork, vibrant colours, and a focus on everyday subjects such as flowers, birds, insects, and small animals. His paintings exuded a sense of warmth, humour, and vitality, capturing the beauty and simplicity of rural life.

One of the most famous stories about Qi Baishi involves an encounter with the renowned American collector, John D. Rockefeller. According to legend, Rockefeller visited Qi Baishi's studio in Beijing in the 1930s and was so impressed with his works that he offered to buy all of the paintings in the studio. However, Qi Baishi refused, insisting that his paintings were not for sale, as they were like his children.

Instead, he gifted Rockefeller a small painting of a shrimp, which became one of his most prized possessions.

Qi Baishi's legacy continues to endure, with his paintings fetching record prices at auctions and his influence being felt by generations of Chinese artists. His life and work serve as a testament to the power of art to transcend cultural boundaries and touch the hearts of people around the world. We can all learn from the perseverance and dedication of this remarkable artist who overcame so much to share his unique vision with the world.

What houses fall in our third house, Who owns it, who the guests are seated in, and their dignity gives one idea of a clear vision. Our aspirations are encapsulated in our vision, which guides us towards purpose and fulfilment. It's a clear picture of the future we strive to create, fueled by our passion, values, and determination. Our vision inspires us to take action, encouraging innovation and resilience even during challenging times. It acts as a beacon that illuminates the path towards our personal and collective progress.

Self-expression and artistic pursuits are often linked with the 3rd and 5th houses. The 5th house governs talents, hobbies, and activities that bring joy and fulfilment to an individual. As a result, people who have a strong planetary influence in their 5th house or a well-placed lord of the 5th house may show artistic inclinations, such as painting.

The placement of the Moon, Venus, and Mercury in the birth chart can also provide insights into one's artistic potential in Vedic astrology. The Moon represents the mind, emotions, and imagination. A strong and well-placed Moon can enhance artistic sensitivity and creativity, providing the emotional depth necessary for expressive painting.

Mercury rules over communication and the mind, and it has two astrological houses - Gemini and Pisces. Gemini is known for versatility, curiosity, and adaptability, while Pisces is linked to intuition, creativity, and imagination. If someone has their Mercury in either of these two houses, it suggests that they might possess a combination of these traits. For instance, an individual with a Mercury in Gemini or Pisces could be a painter who is highly creative and has an intellectual curiosity. Moreover, they can communicate their ideas effectively through their art.

Ch 19

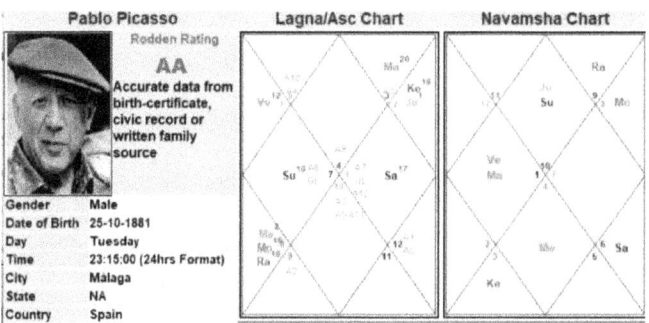

Pablo Ruiz Picasso was a Spanish artist who lived most of his adult life in France. He was a painter, sculptor, printmaker, ceramicist, and theatre designer. He is regarded as one of the most influential artists of the 20th century, co-founding the Cubist movement, inventing constructed sculpture, co-inventing collage, and exploring a wide variety of styles. Some of his most famous works include Les Demoiselles d'Avignon, a proto-Cubist painting, and Guernica, an anti-war painting that depicts the bombing of Guernica by German and Italian air forces during the Spanish Civil War.

Virgo, being the third house, is a problem solver. The owner has Moon and Rahu in the 5th house, and the 11th house lord seated as a guest. How beautifully they painted anti-war to bring peace to humankind.

Ch.20

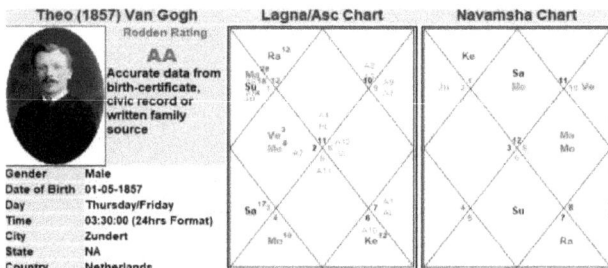

Theodorus van Gogh was a Dutch art dealer and the younger brother of Vincent van Gogh. He was commonly known as Theo. His support for his older brother's artistic ambitions and well-being allowed Vincent to focus solely on painting. As an art dealer, Theo played a crucial role in introducing contemporary French art to the public.

Unfortunately, Theo died at the age of 33, only six months after Vincent's death at the age of 37. However, Theo owned almost all of his brother's artwork. After his death, Theo's widow, Johanna van Gogh-Bonger, worked tirelessly to promote Vincent's work and keep her husband's memory alive. In 1914, Theo van Gogh's remains were buried next to those of his brother Vincent.

Here also, Aries, being a third house sitting on its own, took the responsibility of the brother's painting to promote and keep his work alive. Mars takes responsibility wherever sits. Jupiter became the elder brother Sun and became the owner of the Promoter in this chart.

Ch 21

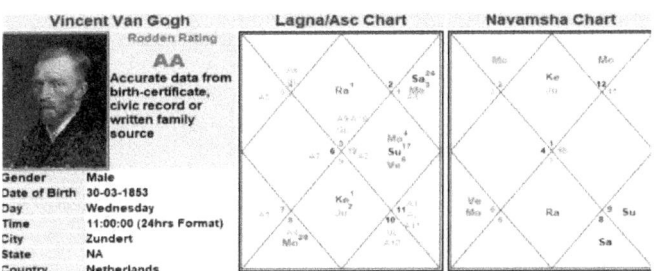

Vincent van Gogh is a Dutch post-impressionist painter whose life and art are deeply intertwined.

Vincent van Gogh experienced periods of deep depression and emotional turmoil, due to his ongoing struggle with mental illness. However, despite the inner turmoil, he had a remarkable talent for art and a strong passion for painting.

One of the most touching aspects of his story is his close relationship with his brother, Theo van Gogh, who provided not only brotherly support but also financial support throughout Vincent's life, enabling him to pursue his artistic goals.

Vincent's artistic journey was characterized by periods of intense creativity and productivity, during which he produced many of his most iconic works, such as "Starry Night," "Sunflowers," and "The Bedroom." However, his mental health issues continued to worsen, leading to moments of despair and anguish.

Despite his struggles, Vincent remained devoted to his art and found comfort and purpose in painting the world around him. His unique style, which featured bold colours, expressive brushwork, and emotive landscapes, continues to captivate audiences worldwide.

Sadly, Vincent van Gogh's life ended prematurely when he committed suicide at the age of 37. However, his legacy lives on through his art, which continues to inspire and move people to this day. Vincent's story serves as a poignant reminder of the profound impact that art can have on the human spirit.

The third house, the Sun, is positioned in the tenth house of Pisces, alongside exalted Venus and Mars, and whenever there is a connection between the third house and Pisces Moon, Venus, and Mercury, then it is believed that the individual in question is likely to possess artistic talents. This suggests that such a person may have a natural inclination towards creative pursuits and may excel in fields such as painting, music, dance, or any other art form that allows them to express themselves creatively.

Ch 22

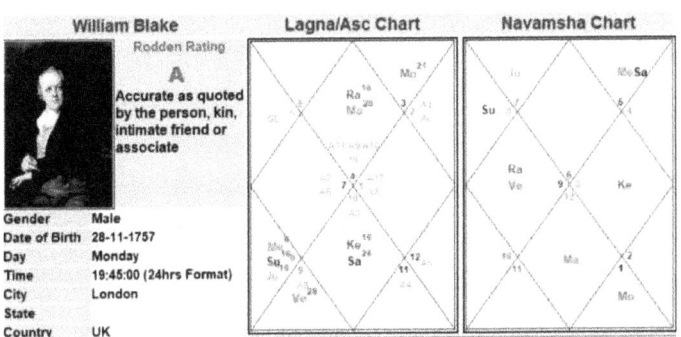

To see a world in a grain of sand and heaven in a wild flower
Hold infinity in the palm of your hand and eternity in an hour.

William Blake was an English poet, painter, and printmaker who lived from 28 November 1757 to 12 August 1827. Although he was largely unrecognised during his lifetime, he is now considered to be a seminal figure in the history of poetry and visual art of the Romantic Age. He referred to his "prophetic works," which 20th-century critic Northrop Frye said formed "what is in proportion to its merits the least read body of poetry in the English language." Blake lived in London his entire life, except for three years spent in Felpham, during which time he produced a diverse and symbolically rich collection of works that embraced the imagination as "the body of God" or "human existence itself."

Blake was a pioneering artist who explored diverse painting and printing techniques. He devised his own approach to relief etching, illuminated printing, which enabled him to produce both text and images on the same plate. This method imparted his paintings with a unique, almost otherworldly appearance.

It is worth noting that Mercury, being lord of the third position, is posited with the sun and Jupiter, making Buddhaaditya Raj yog. He has multiple talents.

Author

Successful writers may have a strength in mercury related to natural expressions of the Kumar. Mercury is in the 3rd house from Chandra, which represents emotional communication, instruction, description, teamwork, administration, management, announcement, publication, reporting, explanation, conversation, lyrics, and messaging.

Mercury governs communication and thought processes. Pisces is linked to abstract thinking and imagination, while Gemini is associated with versatility and linguistic skills, both of which are essential for poetry.

Ch 23

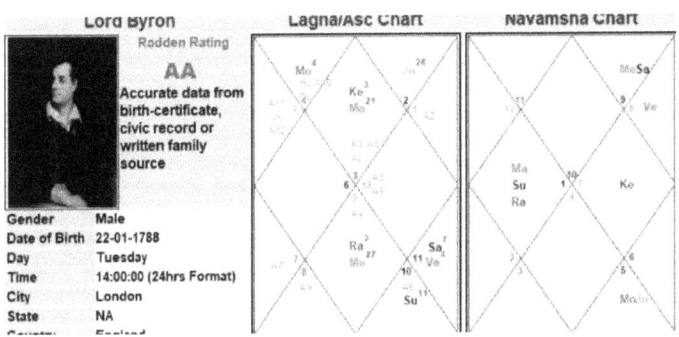

"In secret we met -
In silence I grieve,
That thy heart could forget,
Thy spirit deceive.
If I should meet thee
After long years,
How should I greet thee? -
With silence and tears"
— Lord Byron

Lord Byron, whose full name was George Gordon Byron, was a renowned British poet and a key figure in the Romantic movement. He was born on January 22, 1788, in London, and was the son of Captain John "Mad Jack" Byron and Catherine Gordon. At the age of ten, upon the death of his great-uncle, William Byron, he inherited his great-uncle's title and became the 6th Baron Byron. Byron's personal life was as captivating as his literary works. He was known for his flamboyant lifestyle, passionate relationships, and scandalous behaviour.

His affairs, particularly with married women such as Lady Caroline Lamb and his half-sister Augusta Leigh, were the subject of much gossip and controversy.

skyrocketed with the publication of "Childe Harold's Pilgrimage" in 1812. The semi-autobiographical narrative poem follows the travels and reflections of a young man who is disillusioned with society. The poem brought Byron almost instant fame and established him as one of the leading poets of his time.

Some of Byron's significant literary works include "Manfred" (1817), a dramatic poem that delves into the themes of guilt and redemption; "Don Juan" (1819-1824), a satirical epic poem that narrates the protagonist's escapades; and "The Corsair" (1814), a romantic narrative poem set in the Mediterranean.

In addition to his literary accomplishments, Byron was renowned for his active participation in various political and social movements. He was a vocal advocate for the independence of Greece and ultimately lost his life in Greece while supporting the Greek War of Independence against the Ottoman Empire. Byron's exciting life, intense poetry, and untimely death have all contributed to his legacy as one of the most influential figures of the Romantic era.

Third Lord Sun in Eighth House: After going through transformation or defamation, his poetic talents brought sudden fame, and he became the leading poet of his time.

His poetry is known for its romanticism, passion, and rebelliousness. He often explores themes of love, nature, and the struggle of individuals against societal norms. Byron's writing style uses vivid imagery, intense emotions, and lyrical language to captivate readers, inspiring a sense of longing, sadness, and defiance. His works combine classical influences with a modern sensibility, making a significant impact on English literature.

Ch 24

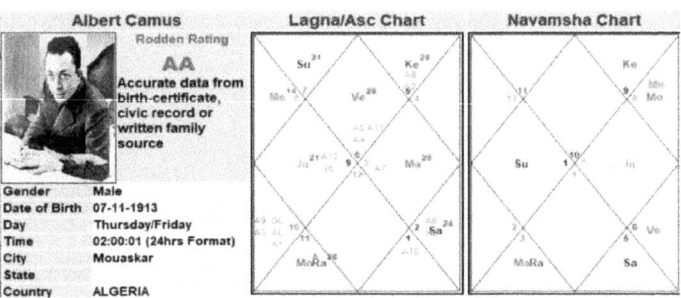

Albert Camus (7 November 1913 – 4 January 1960) was a French author, journalist, philosopher, political activist, and world federalist. He received the Nobel Prize in Literature in 1957 when he was only 44 years old, making him the second-youngest recipient in history. Camus' notable works include The Stranger, The Plague, The Myth of Sisyphus, The Fall, and The Rebel. Albert Camus (7 November 1913 – 4 January 1960) was a French author, journalist, philosopher, political activist, and world federalist. He received the Nobel Prize in Literature in 1957 when he was only 44 years old, making him the second-youngest recipient in history. Camus' notable works include The Stranger, The Plague, The Myth of Sisyphus, The Fall, and The Rebel.

One of his literary works begins with the sentence "My mother died yesterday. in the book "The Stranger". In the above chart, the third house is Scorpio, where the 10th lord . Mercury is positioned. Therefore, his thoughts come from

Scorpio as the house of death. Mother (moon) eleventh house lord. This book brings him Nobel Award.

The story is about a French Algerian man named Meursault who attends his mother's funeral and then finds himself involved in a series of events that eventually lead him to stand trial and get convicted of murder. The novel is considered a classic of existentialist literature because it delves into themes such as the absurdity of human existence, the indifference of the universe, and the individual's struggle to find meaning in life.

Kalidas

In ancient times, a king lived near the city of Ujjain in India. The king had a daughter named Vidyottama who was beautiful and intelligent and was proud of her knowledge. She often belittled the wise men in her father's court, causing them to resent her, although they dared not show it. One day, some wise men stumbled upon a curious sight in the forest. They saw a handsome young man sitting on the top of a tall tree, attempting to chop off the branch he was sitting on. The wise men concluded that he was a great fool, and it turned out that he was none other than Kalidasa. The wise men saw an opportunity to use him to take revenge on Vidyottama.

Vidyottama was of marriageable age and had made up her mind to only marry a man who was more knowledgeable than her. The wise men brought the proposal to the king, and told him that Kalidasa was a learned man who had taken a vow of silence for a month, which was known as maun-vrat. This vow was thought to bring purity of speech and mind and was practiced by many sages back then. The king was impressed by the young man's looks and the praises he received from the wise men in his court. However, Vidyottama insisted on testing his knowledge herself. So, a debate was arranged where Vidyottama and Kalidasa would communicate only through gestures.

When the princess raised her index finger, Kalidasa quickly responded by showing two fingers, thinking that Vidyottama was trying to poke him in the eye. However, she had actually meant that God is one without a second. The wise interpretation of Kalidasa's answer was that truth has two parts: the supreme God and the individual soul. Vidyottama was impressed by his wisdom. She then showed her five fingers to indicate the five senses. Kalidasa thought she was about to hit him, so he showed his fist. Vidyottama interpreted this to mean that controlling the five senses could lead to ultimate greatness. Satisfied, she agreed to marry Kalidasa.

Shortly after their wedding, a camel growled outside their palace one night. When the princess asked what it was, she expected a wise answer from her husband. However, Kalidasa stuttered while trying to say the word camel in Sanskrit (usher). Vidyottama realized that Kalidasa was not a learned man but a fool, and she banished him from their palace. Heartbroken, Kalidasa was about to take his own life. He was a devotee of Kali, and he prayed to her for wisdom. With the blessings of the goddess, Kalidasa was gifted with knowledge and wit. He went on to become one of the greatest Sanskrit poets of all time (mahakavi) and one of the "nine jewels" of King Vikramaditya's court.

Ch 25

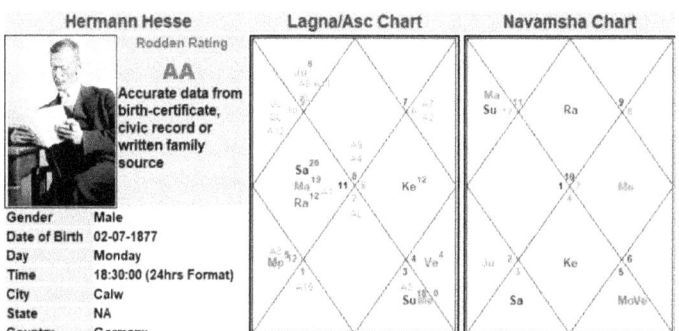

"When someone seeks," said Siddhartha, "then it easily happens that his eyes see only the thing that he seeks, and he is able to find nothing, to take in nothing because he always thinks only about the thing he is seeking, because he has one goal, because he is obsessed with his goal. Seeking means: having a goal. But finding means: being free, being open, having no goal." — Herman Hesse, Siddhartha

Hermann Karl Hesse, a German-Swiss poet, novelist, and painter, is best known for his works such as Demian, Steppenwolf, Siddhartha, and The Glass Bead Game. Each of his works delves into the search for authenticity, self-knowledge, and spirituality of an individual. In 1946, Hesse was awarded the Nobel Prize in Literature.

He was awarded the Nobel Prize for Literature in 1946. Best known for writing 'Steppenwolf', 'Siddhartha', and 'The Glass Bead Game'. He was awarded the Nobel Prize for Literature in 1946. Best known for writing 'Steppenwolf', 'Siddhartha', and 'The Glass Bead Game'.

Gemini is the lord of the 8th house and is in its own house. It is accompanied by the 10th house lord, Sun. All of Gemini's writings explore fears and desires in intricate detail while avoiding ornamental language. He often incorporates elements of mysticism, meditation, and mindfulness in his narratives. His protagonists often embark on physical and spiritual journeys to discover their true selves and break free from societal constraints.

Poet

Legend has it that Kabir, a mystic poet, and saint from the 15th century, was born to Muslim parents but was raised by a Hindu family. Hindus and Muslims both revere him for his teachings on spirituality and the unity of God. Kabir emphasized throughout his life that religious divisions were futile and that God is one.

Kabir once encountered a group of Brahmins who questioned his religious identity. In response, he composed a powerful poem that challenged the rigid boundaries of caste and creed. His message was centred around the idea that the same divine essence flowed through all beings and that true devotion transcended outward labels. Kabir's wisdom was inspiring, and many people from diverse backgrounds became his disciples, drawn to his message of universal love and spiritual harmony.

That the following factors may influence poetic abilities:

1. A strong and unaffected Mercury in the birth chart.

2. A strong Moon which signifies deep connection and emotional expression.

3. A harmonious placement of Venus.

4. A well-placed Jupiter which indicates a broad-minded approach to life.

5. Planets in or aspecting the 5th house, as well as the condition of its ruler.

6. Certain Nakshatras in Vedic astrology, such as Rohini, Hasta, and Swati.

Ch 26

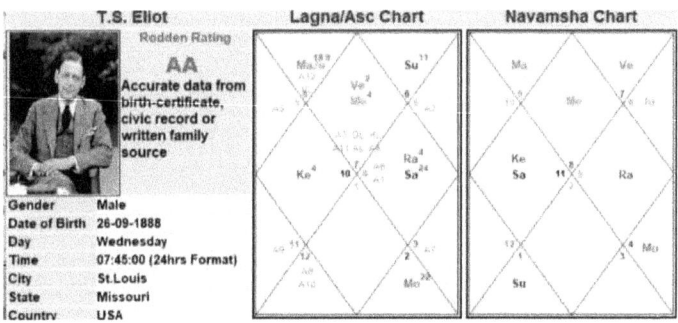

Thomas Stearns Eliot was an accomplished poet, essayist, publisher, playwright, literary critic, and editor. He is widely regarded as one of the greatest poets of the 20th century and a key figure in Modernist poetry in the English language. His unique writing style, use of language, and verse structure brought new life to English poetry. Besides his poetry, he is also well known for his critical essays, which challenged and reevaluated long-held cultural beliefs.

According to the chart mentioned above, Venus and Mercury are in the Ascendant. Jupiter, the third lord, is in the second house along with Mars, the first and second lord.

Eliot's poems are known for their sudden changes in tone, shifting between lyrical, satirical, and philosophical modes. His work delves into the concepts of time, memory, and nonlinear narratives.

Ch 27

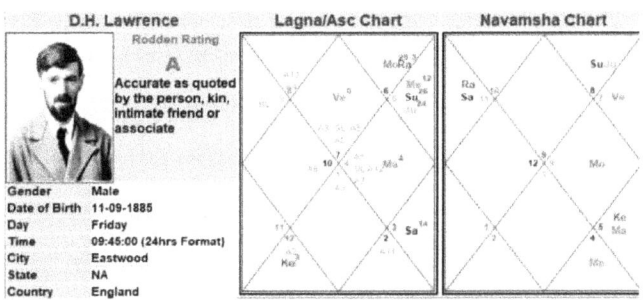

David Herbert Lawrence (11 September 1885 – 2 March 1930) was an English author who wrote novels, poetry, plays, essays, literary criticism, and paintings under the pen name D. H. Lawrence. In his extensive collection of works, Lawrence examined and criticized the negative impacts of modernity and industrialization on human life. He delved into topics such as emotional well-being, energy, spontaneity, and human instinct.

Jupiter, being the owner of the third house, posited with the 11th house with sun and mercury, makes one proficient in his endeavours. His poems often exhibit a strong affinity with the natural world, with recurring themes of yearning, longing, and the pursuit of spiritual fulfilment. Lawrence's language is frequently passionate and grounded, conveying an immediacy and authenticity that are characteristic of his work. He employs unconventional forms of free verse and experimental structures to express the complexities of the human experience, challenging traditional notions of love, identity, and society.

Ch 28

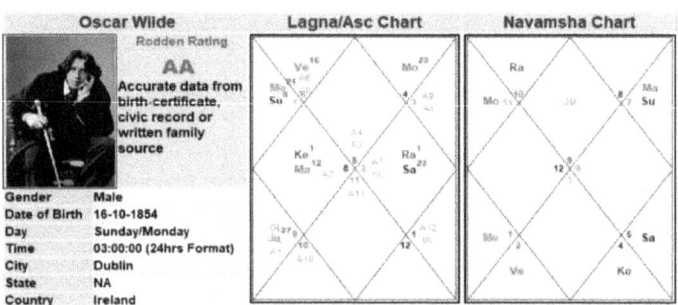

Oscar Fingal O'Flaherty Wills Wilde (16 October 1854 – 30 November 1900) was a celebrated Irish poet and playwright. He wrote in various forms throughout the 1880s and became one of the most renowned playwrights in London in the early 1890s. Wilde is famously known for his sharp and witty epigrams, his plays, including The Importance of Being Earnest, and his novel, The Picture of Dorian Gray. Unfortunately, he faced a criminal conviction for gross indecency for homosexual acts, which is a sad episode in his life.

Oscar Wilde was a renowned writer who was known for his distinctive writing style. He was highly skilled in the use of language and often employed clever wordplay, irony, and satire to create his works. Wilde's writing was characterized by his ability to poke fun at societal conventions and norms, using his wit to highlight the absurdities of everyday life. Sun and Mercury in Libra govern his own vision. This use of humour and sarcasm made his writing highly entertaining and engaging, but it also served a deeper purpose. By exposing the flaws and shortcomings of society, Wilde's writing aimed to bring about social change and provoke critical thinking among his readers. The ascendent lord and eleventh lord in the third house was very successful in his era.

Orator

The art of public speaking is one of the most revered skills in the world, and there are many theories on what makes a great orator. According to astrological beliefs, a strong Mercury and third house in one's birth chart can be the key to unlocking this elusive talent. By tapping into the power of the planets, you can enhance your public speaking abilities and become a master of the art of persuasion.

Ch 29

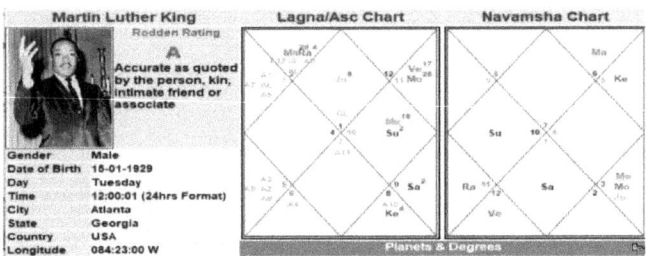

Martin Luther King Jr. was an American Christian minister, political philosopher, and civil rights activist. He was one of the most prominent leaders in the civil rights movement from 1955 until his assassination in 1968. As the son of early civil rights activist and minister Martin Luther King Sr., King worked towards advancing civil rights for people of colour in the United States. He used nonviolent resistance and civil disobedience against Jim Crow laws and other forms of legalized discrimination.

In his famous "I Have a Dream" speech delivered on August 28, 1963, during the March on Washington for Jobs and Freedom, Martin Luther King Jr. shared his vision for racial equality and justice in the United States. Some noteworthy phrases from the speech include:

"I have a dream that one day this nation will rise up and live out the true meaning of its creed: 'We hold these truths to be self-evident, that all men are created equal.'"

"I have a dream that my four little children will one day live in a nation where they will not be judged by the colour of their skin but by the content of their character."

"Let freedom ring! And when this happens, when we allow freedom to ring, when we let it ring from every village and every hamlet, from every state and every city, we will be able to speed up that day when all of God's children, black men and white men, Jews and Gentiles, Protestants and Catholics, will be able to join hands and sing in the words of the old Negro spiritual: 'Free at last! Free at last! Thank God Almighty, we are free at last!'"

Third-house Lord Mercury is posited in the 10th house of Capricorn with the sun. Centre-stage Surya's brightly charismatic confidence radiates in Shani's rashi.

Sun conjunct Mercury makes self-confident. It is the mercury that gives him his legendary speech, which starts with " I have a dream."The third house lord IN the 10th house makes one kingmaker. During the Mercury Mahadasa, he got the Nobel Peace Prize at the age of 35 in 1946.

Ch 30

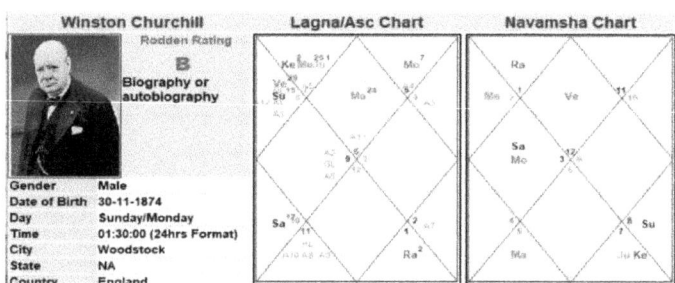

Sir Winston Leonard Spencer Churchill was a prominent British statesman, soldier, and writer. He served as the Prime Minister of the United Kingdom twice, first from 1940 to 1945 during the Second World War and again from 1951 to 1955. He was a Member of Parliament (MP) for most of his career, serving from 1900 to 1964 and representing a total of five constituencies, except for two years between 1922 and 1924. Churchill was ideologically an adherent to economic liberalism and imperialism and was a member of the Conservative Party, which he led from 1940 to 1955. He was also a member of the Liberal Party from 1904 to 1924.

Scorpio sun in the third house with Venus confidently harmonious, radiantly diplomatic, and graciously creative in politics and finance. Dispositor in ascendent gives name and fame in his own era,

Ch 31

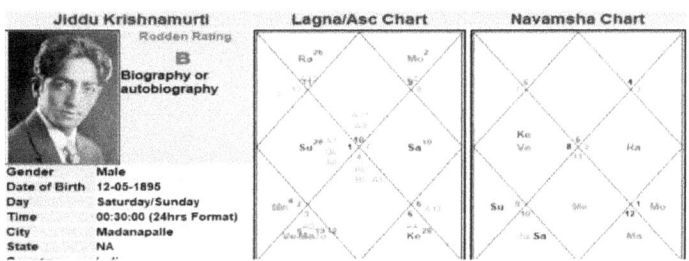

Jiddu Krishnamurti (11 May 1895 – 17 February 1986) was an Indian philosopher, writer, speaker, and spiritual figure. As a child, he was adopted by members of the Theosophical tradition and raised to become a World Teacher. However, Krishnamurti rejected this position as he grew older and distanced himself from the religious movement that came with it. Instead, he spent the rest of his life speaking to groups and individuals around the world, with many of his talks published in books such as The First and Last Freedom (1954) and Commentaries on Living (1956-60). Krishnamurti emphasized the importance of choiceless awareness, psychological inquiry, and freedom from religious, spiritual, and cultural conditioning. He believed that "truth is a pathless land" and advised against following any doctrine, discipline, teacher, guru, or authority, including himself. Despite his rejection of the World Teacher role, Krishnamurti's supporters have established non-profit foundations in India, Britain, and the United States to oversee independent schools based on his educational philosophy. His thousands of talks, group and individual discussions, and writings are still distributed in a variety of media formats and languages. Krishnamurti delivered his last public talk in January 1986, a month before his death at his home in Ojai, California.

In the given context, the positioning of Gemini in the astrological chart assumes a significant role in conjunction with the 12th lord Jupiter and Venus. While Jupiter symbolizes the spiritual aspect of an individual, Gemini's position in the sixth house brings forth a logical and analytical approach to the practical matters related to one's individuality. This combination results in a unique balance between an individual's spiritual and practical aspects, allowing them to navigate through various situations with clarity and purpose..

The power of name

Namkaran, also known as Namakarana Sanskar or Namakaranam, is the traditional naming ceremony for a newborn baby in Hindu culture. It is regarded as one of the significant samskaras (sacraments) in Hinduism.

The Namkaran ceremony is a significant event in Hinduism, where family members select a name for the newborn based on cultural or religious significance, family tradition, or personal preference. Before the ceremony, the baby and mother may undergo a purification ritual. During the ceremony, the father whispers the chosen name into the baby's ear and a mixture of honey and ghee is applied to the baby's lips. The occasion is celebrated with feasting and blessings from family and friends. The chosen name is believed to influence the child's personality and future prospects.

The power of a name goes beyond its mere syllables. It serves as a vessel of our identity, carrying the essence of our heritage and the aspirations our parents had for us. A name can greatly influence perceptions, affect decisions, and evoke emotions. It serves as a bridge between the tangible world and the realm of ideas, enabling individuals to connect with one another across time and space..

Names are considered very important in certain cultures, as they are believed to have the ability to bring good luck or bad luck to the person who bears them. A family name can carry the weight of the past, present, and future generations, which can be a source of pride or a burden depending on how it is perceived. Names are deeply personal but also communal. They anchor us within our families, communities, and societies. They are how we introduce ourselves, how we're recognized, and how we're remembered. They reflect culture, history, and tradition, conveying meanings and symbolizing virtues.

Story of Dashyu Ratnakar

In ancient times, there was a notorious bandit named Ratnakar who lived in the dense forests of India. He was feared for his ruthlessness and cruelty, and he resorted to a life of crime to sustain his family. Despite his nefarious deeds, Ratnakar was not entirely devoid of conscience. Deep down, he felt guilty about his actions, but the allure of wealth and power kept him bound to his life of crime.

One day, while Ratnakar was attempting to rob a traveller, he encountered a revered sage who remained calm and unperturbed by his threats. Intrigued by the sage's composure, Ratnakar questioned him about his unwavering demeanour. The sage responded with wisdom and compassion, explaining the true path to inner peace and fulfilment.

Moved by the sage's words, Ratnakar was overcome with remorse and realisation. He realised the gravity of his sins and the emptiness of his existence. In a moment of transformation, he fell at the sage's feet and begged for forgiveness.

The sage, moved by Ratnakar's sincerity, bestowed upon him a new purpose and identity. He instructed Ratnakar to renounce his life of crime and seek redemption through penance and devotion. He gave Ratnakar a new name - Valmiki, meaning "the one born of the ant-hill."

Embracing his new identity, Valmiki embarked on a spiritual journey of self-discovery and transformation. He retreated deep into the forest, living in solitude and contemplation. Through years of meditation and introspection, he purified his heart and mind, transcending his former self.

As time passed, Valmiki emerged from his seclusion as a revered sage and poet. He composed the epic poem Ramayana, which narrated the timeless tale of Lord Rama's life and virtues. Through his literary masterpiece, Valmiki conveyed the eternal principles of dharma, righteousness, and the triumph of good over evil.

The story of Dasyu Ratnakar, who became the sage Valmiki, serves as a powerful reminder of the human capacity for transformation and redemption. It teaches us that no matter how deep one's fall, there is always hope for renewal and enlightenment through sincere repentance and spiritual awakening.

The Story of Ajamila

AjmilaIn ancient India, there was a man named Ajamila. He was once a devout Brahmin, but later, he succumbed to worldly temptations and led a life full of sin and immorality. At the end of his life, as he lay on his deathbed, Ajamila was filled with fear and regret for all the wrongs he had done.

In a moment of desperation, he called out the name of his youngest son, Narayana, which was also a name for the Supreme Lord. What Ajamila didn't know was that this single utterance of the divine name had the power to redeem his soul. The divine messengers, who were present in the celestial realms, heard his plea and were moved by the sincerity of his repentance. Lord Vishnu, the Supreme Lord, dispatched his messengers to take Ajamila to the abode of eternal bliss.

Ajamila's story serves as a testament to the transformative power of devotion and the boundless mercy of the divine. It shows that even in the darkest moments of despair, the utterance of a divine name can bring redemption and liberation from the cycle of birth and death.

In ancient India, there was a man named Ajamila. He was once a devout Brahmin, but later, he succumbed to worldly temptations and led a life full of sin and immorality. At the end of his life, as he lay on his deathbed, Ajamila was filled with fear and regret for all the wrongs he had done.

In a moment of desperation, he called out the name of his youngest son, Narayana, which was also a name for the Supreme Lord. What Ajamila didn't know was that this single utterance of the divine name had the power to redeem his soul. The divine messengers, who were present in the celestial realms, heard his plea and were moved by the sincerity of his repentance. Lord Vishnu, the Supreme Lord, dispatched his messengers to take Ajamila to the abode of eternal bliss.

Ajamila's story serves as a testament to the transformative power of devotion and the boundless mercy of the divine. It shows that even in the darkest moments of despair, the utterance of a divine name can bring redemption and liberation from the cycle of birth and death..

The Story of Mirabai

During the golden age of Indian mysticism, in Rajasthan's palaces and bazaars, lived a princess who had only one love in her heart—the love of the divine. Despite being born into privilege and luxury, Mirabai's soul yearned for something beyond material riches. From an early age, she found solace in devotional melodies and poetry of the soul.

Despite her family's protests and society's scorn, Mirabai's love for Lord Krishna burned bright and unyielding. She danced through the moonlit nights, her voice soaring with the ecstasy of divine union. Through every trial and tribulation, she clung to the name of her beloved Lord, finding strength and solace in the depths of her devotion.

Mirabai's life was a tapestry woven with threads of love and longing, devotion, and surrender. Her poetry echoed through the ages, a testimony to the transformative power of the divine name. For Mirabai, chanting Krishna's name was not just a ritual but a lifeline, a source of boundless joy and eternal communion with the beloved. During the golden age of Indian mysticism, in Rajasthan's palaces and bazaars, lived a princess who had only one love in her heart - the love of the divine. Despite being born into privilege and luxury, Mirabai's soul yearned for something beyond material riches. From an early age, she found solace in the devotional melodies and poetry of the soul.

Despite her family's protests and society's scorn, Mirabai's love for Lord Krishna burned bright and unyielding. She danced through the moonlit nights, her voice soaring with the ecstasy of divine union. Through every trial and tribulation, she clung to the name of her beloved Lord, finding strength and solace in the depths of her devotion.

Mirabai's life was a tapestry woven with threads of love and longing, devotion, and surrender. Her poetry echoed through the ages, a testimony to the transformative power of the divine name. For Mirabai, chanting Krishna's name was not just a ritual but a lifeline, a source of boundless joy and eternal communion with the beloved.

The Story of Tulsidas

In the lush green landscapes of 16th-century India, amidst the soft whispers of sacred hymns and the sweet fragrance of marigold blossoms, there lived a saint whose words would echo through the corridors of time. Tulsidas, a humble devotee of Lord Rama, walked the rugged path of devotion with unwavering faith and determination.

Born into a world full of challenges and turmoil, Tulsidas found solace in the timeless tales of the Ramayana. Through chanting Lord Rama's name, he overcame the limitations of his earthly existence and found refuge in the boundless ocean of divine grace. Amidst the trials and tribulations of life, Tulsidas sought comfort in the company of his beloved Lord and penned verses that would illuminate the path of seekers for centuries to come.

Through his epic poem, the Ramcharitmanas, Tulsidas captured the essence of divine love and sacrifice, inspiring generations to embrace the teachings of righteousness and compassion. His life was a testament to the transformative power of devotion, a beacon of light in a world shrouded in darkness.

The Story of Prahlad

In the ancient mythical realm of India, gods and demons would often engage in epic battles. In this world, there was a prince named Prahlad, the son of the demon king Hiranyakashipu. Despite the environment of oppression and tyranny, Prahlad was a beacon of light whose faith was unyielding. He had been devoted to Lord Vishnu, the sustainer of the universe, since childhood and continued to chant His name with unwavering devotion despite his father's wrath and the demons' hostile schemes.

Prahlad's heart was set ablaze with divine love, and he remained steadfast in his faith despite the chaos around him. Due to his unwavering devotion, he invoked the protection of Lord Vishnu, who appeared in the form of Narasimha, the half-man, half-lion incarnation. Narasimha roared with such ferocity that it shook the heavens and earth, vanquishing Prahlad's oppressors and delivering him from the jaws of death.

It reminds us that even in the darkest of times, the chanting of the divine name can bestow divine protection and grace.

Greek mythology

In Greek mythology, names carry significant weight beyond just being labels. They embody the essence of identity, power and destiny. The names of characters in Greek mythology are not arbitrary; they often reflect the bearer's character, lineage or divine essence. Let's explore the importance of names in Greek mythology through a descriptive lens.

In the pantheon of the Olympian gods, each deity has a name that encapsulates their domain and attributes. Zeus, the ruler of the heavens and king of the gods, derives his name from the Greek word "Dios," which means "sky" or "daylight." His name evokes the majesty and authority that befits his role as the chief deity.

Similarly, Athena, the goddess of wisdom and warfare, derives her name from "Athena," the ancient Greek city where she was revered as a patron deity. Her name signifies intellect, strategy, and the valor of battle.

Beyond the realm of the gods, names remain significant for mortal heroes and creatures alike. Achilles, the greatest of the Greek warriors in the Trojan War, derives his name from the Greek word "akhos," which means "pain" or "grief." His name foreshadows the tragic fate that awaits him, as he meets his demise at the hands of Paris, guided by the arrow of Apollo.

Even creatures of myth and legend bear names that reflect their nature and origins. The Chimera, a fearsome monster with the body of a lion, the head of a goat, and the tail of a serpent, derives its name from the Greek word "khimaira," which means "she-goat." Its name embodies the monstrous fusion of disparate elements, symbolising chaos and destruction.

In Greek mythology, names possess a power beyond their literal meanings; they control fate and destiny. The hero Odysseus, renowned for his wit and resourcefulness, hides his true identity under the name "Nobody" to outsmart the Cyclops Polyphemus. By manipulating the power of his name, Odysseus secures his escape from the giant's clutches.

Names have a significant role in marking the lineage and heritage of individuals by carrying the legacies of their ancestors and gods. The descendants of noble families, like the House of Atreus or the House of Perseus, bear names that evoke the glory and tragedy of their family's history. Names in Greek mythology are imbued with profound significance, reflecting the essence of identity, power, and destiny. They shape the narratives of gods, heroes, and creatures alike, weaving a tapestry of myth and legend that endures through the ages.

In chienese Astrology

In ancient China, a young couple eagerly awaited the birth of their first child and sought the guidance of Master Li, a renowned astrologer, to choose an auspicious name for their baby. The astrologer advised them on the significance of selecting a name that resonated harmoniously with the celestial forces governing their child's destiny. In Chinese, each character in a name carries its own vibrational energy that can either harmonise or clash with an individual's astrological chart.

The couple meticulously crafted a name for their child, ensuring that each character symbolised prosperity, longevity, and virtue, aligning with the positive traits indicated in their child's astrological chart. As the child grew, he embodied the qualities symbolised by each character in his name, becoming a person of integrity, wisdom, and success.

Years later, the young man encountered an old sage deep in meditation atop a mist-shrouded mountain. The young man introduced himself by his full name, and to his amazement, the sage recognised the harmonious energy of his name. The sage remarked that the young man's name reflected his true nature and potential, inspiring him to fulfil his destiny and leave an indelible mark on the world.

The story illustrates the importance of choosing an auspicious name in Chinese. An auspicious name can unlock one's innate potential and guide one towards a fulfilling and prosperous life.

Amin

In a busy city along the banks of the Nile, a devout couple lived eagerly waiting for the birth of their first child. Being devout Muslims, they wanted to choose a name that would reflect their child's faith and identity in accordance with Islamic teachings.

The couple sought advice from the local Imam, a learned scholar who was well-versed in Islamic jurisprudence and traditions. They shared their hopes and aspirations, expressing their desire for a name that would bring blessings and guidance throughout their child's life.

The Imam listened attentively and began to offer guidance, drawing upon the Quran's wisdom and the Prophet Muhammad's traditions (peace be upon him). He explained that in Islam, names are not just labels but are imbued with spiritual significance, reflecting the attributes of Allah and the teachings of Islam.

The couple and the Imam explored the meanings and symbolism of various Islamic names, searching for one that would resonate with their faith and aspirations. After much contemplation and prayer, they settled upon the name "Amin," which means "faithful" and "trustworthy" in Arabic.

As years passed, young Amin grew in wisdom and stature, embodying the virtues symbolised by his name. He devoted himself to the teachings of Islam, striving to uphold the principles of honesty, integrity, and compassion in all his endeavours.

One day, Amin met a wise Sufi mystic who recognised the depth of his character and the purity of his heart. "Your name reflects the essence of your soul," the mystic remarked.

Inspired by the mystic's words, Amin redoubled his efforts to deepen his connection to his faith and serve humanity with humility and compassion. Through his exemplary conduct and dedication to Islam, he became a source of inspiration and guidance for others, embodying the timeless teachings of the Prophet Muhammad (peace be upon him) and the transformative power of a name rooted in faith and piety.

This story illustrates the profound importance of names in Islam and their role in shaping an individual's faith, character, and destiny. It highlights the belief that a name aligned with Islamic teachings can serve as a source of blessings and guidance throughout one's life journey.

Sufism

In Sufism, the mystical branch of Islam, names hold profound significance as they are seen as vehicles for spiritual transformation and connection to the divine. The choice of a name in Sufism is often guided by the belief in the sacred power of words and the potential for a name to shape one's spiritual journey.

In the heart of a bustling bazaar in ancient Persia lived a humble artisan known for his skill in crafting intricate carpets adorned with mystical symbols and verses from the Quran. Despite his outward simplicity, the artisan possessed a deep longing for spiritual truth and enlightenment.

One day, an artisan sat in his workshop, deep in thought, when a wise Sufi master visited him. The Sufi master was renowned for his wisdom and had come to offer spiritual guidance to the artisan. As they talked, the Sufi master explained the importance of names in Sufism. In this tradition, names are not just labels but carry the essence of divine attributes and qualities. By repeating and contemplating these sacred names, Sufis seek spiritual illumination and union with the divine.

The artisan was moved by the Sufi master's words and expressed his desire to follow the path of Sufism and find a spiritual name to guide him. The Sufi master invited him on a pilgrimage to a sacred shrine in the mountains. During their journey, the master taught the artisan about love, devotion, and selflessness. They arrived at the shrine, a place of tranquillity and divine presence, where the master bestowed upon the artisan a new name – "Rumi," meaning "the beloved" in Persian. The master explained that the name carried the vibration of divine love and served as a reminder of the eternal bond between the soul and its Creator.

Rumi returned to his workshop with a renewed sense of purpose and devotion with his new name. He wove carpets and chanted sacred verses, seeking to awaken the hearts of all who beheld his creations to the beauty and majesty of divine love. Over time, Rumi's name became synonymous with spiritual enlightenment and poetic inspiration. His verses transcended time and space, touching the hearts of seekers across the ages. His life journey exemplified the transformative power of a name rooted in Sufi tradition and the boundless depths of divine love.

Western culture

Names hold a significant place in Western culture as they are often viewed as a reflection of one's personal identity, family heritage, and individuality. Choosing a name for a child is a deeply personal decision for parents, influenced by cultural, familial, and personal factors. Let me tell you a story that explores the importance of names in Western culture:

In a beautiful village surrounded by rolling hills and lush greenery, a young couple named Sarah and David were eagerly waiting for the arrival of their first child. As they anticipated the joyous moment of birth, they pondered over the perfect name for their newborn, realizing the weighty responsibility that came with their decision.

Sarah and David belonged to families rich in tradition and history, with each name carrying its significance and legacy. Sarah's family had a long lineage of strong, resilient women, while David's ancestors were renowned for their integrity and courage.

As they sat together in their cosy cottage, surrounded by the warmth of flickering candlelight, Sarah and David embarked on a journey of exploration and contemplation, seeking a name that would honour their heritage and embody their hopes and dreams for their child.

They delved into family archives, poring over old photographs and dusty genealogy records, uncovering their ancestors' stories and the names passed down through generations. Each name held a tale of triumph, tragedy, resilience, and perseverance, weaving a tapestry of family history and cultural identity.

During their search, Sarah and David came across the name "Eleanor," a name steeped in medieval tradition and noble lineage. Derived from the Greek words meaning "bright" and "shining," Eleanor exuded a sense of grace, strength, and luminosity that resonated deeply with the couple.

With hearts brimming with anticipation and reverence, Sarah and David welcomed their newborn daughter into the world, cradling her in their arms with a sense of awe and wonder. As they gazed into her eyes, they knew in their hearts that she was destined to embody the spirit of her namesake, Eleanor, a beacon of light and hope in a world filled with darkness.

As the years passed, Eleanor grew into a young woman of grace and elegance, her name serving as a guiding star on her journey of self-discovery and fulfilment. She embraced her heritage with pride and honour, embodying the virtues of her ancestors and forging her path with courage and conviction.

Through the power of her name, Eleanor became a testament to the importance of identity and heritage in Western culture, a living embodiment of the timeless traditions and values passed down through generations. Her story served as a reminder of the significance of names in shaping our sense of self and connection to the past, present, and future.

The planet Mercury, the third house in Vedic astrology, is the actual controller of Name.

The process of naming a child is determined by the nakshatra (lunar mansion) in which the moon is located in the child's astrological chart. Mercury and the third house can also influence the way in which a person is named.

It has been observed that when Mercury is connected with Rahu, the name tends to be longer, whereas with Ketu, the name is usually shorter. A connection with Jupiter results in a heavy and related divine or weighty name, mercury with moon related to flower, while a connection with Mars can lead to a name associated with bravery or valour. Mercury's association with Saturn is linked to historical events, whereas its connection with the Sun is related to kingly or authoritative figures. It is worth noting that a child's name is often derived from their father's name or incorporates an aspect of their original name.

Mercury often provides a significant clue as to who named a person. If Mercury is connected to the Moon, it is likely that the mother named the person. The father may have given the name if Mercury is connected to the Sun. If Mercury is associated with Jupiter, it could be a pandit or a grandparent who named the person. Similarly, if Mercury is related to Venus, a sister may have named the person, and a brother may have given the name if connected to Mars. If Mercury is linked to Saturn, it is possible that the most senior member of the family named the person. Furthermore, it is worth noting that if Mercury is connected to many planets, the person may have been given different names by different people throughout their life.

In Hindu culture, naming ceremonies are often performed based on the Chandra Nakshatra Pada. It is believed that the name chosen for the child should be based on the auspicious alignment of the stars at the time of their birth. However, upon delving deeper into this practice, it has been observed that the names often end up being related to the planet Mercury. Mercury is associated with communication, intelligence, and quick wit, making it a popular choice for the names of newborns.

Third house lord in different House

First The person may tend to argue and have difficulty maintaining positive relationships with relatives. They may associate with negative individuals and prioritize their interests over others. However, they also demonstrate strong dedication, and their achievements are a result of their own hard work, showcasing their potential for personal growth and self-empowerment. Additionally, they possess bravery, a trait that can help them overcome these challenges.

The nature of the individual's married life may be influenced by the aspect that the owner of the third house casts on the seventh. If the third house owner is either Jupiter or Mercury and the sign in the third house is either Gemini or Sagittarius, it could cause significant problems for the individual's married life. Moreover, if the owner of the third house is associated with or in sambandha with Venus simultaneously, the individual can expect no respite from a marriage that will become a burden. Even if the owner of the third house also owns the second or twelfth house, or an angle, it will still cause problems for the individual in their married life, though the influence will not be as severe.

The person, guided by the third house lord, may find an affinity for music or art. If the owner of the third house shares a friendly relationship with the owner of the ascendant in the first house, the individual can look forward to positive and harmonious relationships with their siblings, neighbours, and colleagues. This connection can foster a sense of optimism and belonging in their social circle. However, it's important to note that the native's mother, if she has an independent profession, may face losses, and she may work in a hospital or asylum. A strongly placed owner of the third house in the first house will lead to the individual's children becoming successful and wealthy. Finally, the person's father may display sensual tendencies.

Second In astrology, the third house's malevolent owner has the potential to decrease the native's longevity, and he may have a stout build. Additionally, this native will not be cordial to his relatives, and he will be poor and unscrupulous. However, the native's intense desire for women and other people's wealth can be channeled into a drive for financial and professional success, inspiring and motivating the individual to overcome life's challenges. Moreover, the major or sub-periods of the third house's owner may cause the native to lose his younger sibling, which can be a painful experience.

However, if the third house has a beneficial owner, the native will become wealthy and powerful through his own efforts. This means that the native will be able to achieve success in life by working hard and smartly. Furthermore, the native's younger sibling will live away from the native's place and be wealthy there, indicating that the sibling may have a successful career or business.

The native's children are likely to be wealthy and well-placed, which can bring joy and happiness to the native's life. Additionally, the native's mother may be extravagant and not friendly, preferring to be alone, which can create some emotional distance between them. On the other hand, the father will enjoy good health and may not have issues with enemies or thieves, which can give him peace of mind. The father will be content with his servants, which shows that he will be satisfied with his work and the people around him.

Third Based on the astrological reading of the individual's birth chart, it is predicted that this person will be born into a family that is highly regarded and respected for their religious beliefs and affiliation with the government. The individual is destined to benefit from government dealings and is expected to possess a fearless attitude, always prepared to take risks in pursuit of their goals. Moreover, their intellectual abilities will be remarkable, and they will be renowned for their written works in the fields of law, philosophy, or religion.

It is predicted that the younger sibling of the individual may have a strained relationship with their father if the owner of the third house is an enemy of the owner of the ninth house. However, the individual will have a close and friendly bond with their younger sibling, and they will benefit from them in various ways.

The spouse of the individual is predicted to be a fortunate, virtuous, and religious person who will bring prosperity and happiness to the individual's life. This is a favourable position concerning the fortune and prosperity of their children, and it is predicted that their elder siblings will have a contented life with their own children and be well-respected in society.

Fourth The native will likely find happiness from his father and other family members. However, he may not have a pleasant relationship with his mother who is introverted and extravagant. It is possible that she may join a secret society, which may create further distance between them.

The native is likely to be financially reckless and may squander away his family's wealth. However, he will be enterprising and earn his own property and vehicles through his efforts. The native will also have diverse interests and maybe a public figure.

Although the native may not pursue traditional education, he will continue to learn and grow through correspondence courses.

The younger sibling of the native is likely to achieve success through their own efforts.

The native's wife may be a source of trouble, but if the owner of the third house is powerful and well-placed in the fourth house, she will achieve wealth and status in life.

Fifth - He will take care of the children of his native, including his brothers and nephews.

His own children will have their aspirations fulfilled and will eventually become wealthy.

He will live a long life and be known for his charitable deeds.

He will continuously strive to gain knowledge.

It's possible that his younger brother may attain a high-ranking position such as a secretary or minister.

The native may also act as a host or emcee at social gatherings.

If a malefic planet affects the third-house owner, his wife is likely to be troublesome and cause difficulties in his life.

Sixth : The person may experience a health issue related to the ear or a chronic illness.

They will acquire property and express animosity towards their maternal uncle and younger sibling.

The individual will have a fondness for their maternal aunt during the major or sub-periods of the owner of the third house.

In the major or sub-periods of the third-house owner, the younger sibling may pass away.

The person will face difficulties from their enemies.

This implies that the younger sibling may pursue a career in the military or medicine.

If there's a connection between the third or eleventh house and the sixth, then Paragraph 7 under the Sixth House should be examined to determine the individual's possible profession.

If a powerful third-house owner is well-placed in the sixth house, the younger sibling may gain wealth, property, and education.

The individual's partner or spouse will travel abroad.

If the third house owner is weak and afflicted but unfavorable, this may still yield positive outcomes for the individual's worldly affairs.

Seventh – The individual will be presented with an opportunity to work for the government.

Despite encountering some health difficulties in their youth, the person will ultimately lead a rewarding life.

The person's significant other will be attractive and potentially come from a diverse cultural background, which can bring depth and variety to their relationship.

Individuals should be cautious of adverse planetary influences on their spouse's behaviour. However, if the planets are favourably aligned, the individual's younger sibling will provide them with support and care.

The individual's mother will be from an intriguing and distinct location, offering a unique perspective on life and culture.

The individual's brother will have the chance to explore the world and gain valuable life experiences.

Eighth –The third house in a birth chart can have significant implications for the native. If the owner of the third house is a weak and afflicted malefic planet, the native may suffer from arm loss or die in childhood. However, if the owner of the third house is powerful and placed in a favourable sign, it can enhance the native's longevity and benefit their wife and children.

During the major or sub-periods of the third-house owner, the death or serious illness of a younger sibling can be predicted. The native's mother may also lose in gambling or speculation. If the third-house owner is well-placed, the native will generally enjoy good health.

If the owner of the third house is placed in the eighth house and contacts the owner of the sixth house, it can result in good financial returns during its major or sub-periods. However, the native may face scandalous allegations or get involved in a criminal case. Troubles can also arise due to a legacy.

Ninth - The quality of the relationship between the natives and their younger siblings is determined by the nature of the third house owner. The relationship will be poor if the owner is very malefic in the chart. On the other hand, if the owner is not malefic, the relationship will be good, and the native will also be a scholar. The younger siblings will live a long, healthy life, inherit property, and prosper. The native will prosper after getting married. There is a possibility that the native's brother-in-law may become a business partner. If the owner of the third house is weak and afflicted and has no beneficial influence, the native's mother will have a good reputation in society and be wealthy. The native's children will earn well through their abilities, entertainment, or speculation. The native may conduct research and write scholarly theses. The native's father may not have a good character.

Tenth- The native will have the goodwill of the government and be affectionate towards their parents. They may not have younger siblings if Mars is weak and unsatisfactorily placed in the chart. If the placement of the owner of the third house is accompanied by Jupiter being badly placed, weak in the chart, or adversely influenced, the native's elder sibling may be childless. The native may join service through self-effort and writing may play a role in their success. They may change their residence due to a transfer in service. The native may be able to write bestsellers that will earn them money and fame, and they will be highly respected. Their wife will be educated, religious, and spiritually inclined. However, she may lose her father during the major or sub-periods of the owner of the third house.

Eleventh -The forecast indicates that the individual in question and their younger sibling are likely to become prosperous and occupy esteemed positions. They will generate income through various channels such as railways, telegraph, radio, and television and will put in efforts to accomplish their financial objectives. The person's siblings will also excel in their respective lives and maintain a strong bond with one another. The person's offspring might be influenced by their younger sibling, who could be employed. However, the person's health may not be up to the mark.

If the owner of the third house is friendly with the owner of the eleventh house and is a powerful planet, the elder sibling of the person in question will be very attached to their own children. The owner of the third house in the eleventh house will also enable the person's father-in-law to earn well from speculation or entertainment, and their spouse will receive a windfall. If the owner of the third house is a beneficial planet, the person's spouse will be religious and enjoy a prosperous life after the birth of their children. However, if the owner of the third house is weak and afflicted and has no beneficial influence, the person's mother will be wealthy and rise high in life.

Twelfth -The younger siblings and friends of the native will be opposed by him. He may exhibit laziness, but he will experience good fortune after his marriage. The native's younger brother or sister may suffer losses or may be associated with a secret society or hospital. Although the younger sibling may be wealthy and well-established, they may leave their native place to live abroad. During the major or sub-periods of the owner of the third house in the twelfth house, the native's father-in-law may fall ill and require hospitalization. The maternal uncle of the native's spouse may go on a long journey, and the native may experience trouble with their ear. If the owner of the third house is a highly malefic planet for the chart and is afflicted in the twelfth house, there is a possibility that one of the native's children may be affected.

Below are descriptions of where the House Lords are placed in the Third House and how it affects their communication style and networking abilities:

An individual with a strong emphasis on personal identity and self-expression in communication and networking may result from having the First House Lord in the Third House. They may appear assertive in their interactions and value their own interests in their communication style.

Second House Lord in Third House: The placement of these individuals may involve linking financial affairs with communication and siblings. They tend to adopt a pragmatic approach when it comes to communication, frequently utilizing it to obtain resources or improve their financial status. Additionally, they may participate in business ventures associated with transportation or communication.

Third House Lord in Third House: The placement can enhance the qualities linked with the third house, such as excellent communication skills, courage, and initiative. People with this placement may excel at expressing themselves and connecting with others, particularly their siblings. They may also thrive in careers related to writing, teaching, or media.

Fourth House Lord in Third House: This placement may influence an individual's communication style and interactions with their siblings, based on family matters and emotional security. People with this placement may prioritise maintaining family connections through communication and have a strong sense of tradition. Furthermore, they may emphasise real estate or property-related communication.

Fifth House Lord in Third House: Those with this placement may prioritise expressing themselves creatively when communicating and networking. They may also have a strong desire to share their ideas and could excel in fields such as education, entertainment, or speculative ventures. Additionally, they may have dynamic and engaging relationships with their siblings.

Sixth House Lord in Third The position of the house could lead to someone who communicates in a way that is influenced by their health, their work in the service industry, and their daily routine. They might possess excellent problem-solving abilities and excel in fields related to healthcare, administration, or service industries. When interacting with their siblings, their communication may revolve around practical matters or daily routines.

Seventh House Lord in Third House: An individual's communication style and interactions with siblings may be influenced by their relationships and partnerships. Within close relationships, they may prioritize diplomacy and harmony in their communication. This placement may place emphasis on business partnerships and negotiations.

Eighth House Lord in Third House: Communication and networking may be areas of interest for those with this placement, which is characterized by a profound and transformative approach.

- Seeking hidden truths and uncovering secrets through communication could be a focus for individuals with this placement.

- Strong intuition may be a hallmark of this placement, potentially leading to success in fields such as psychology, counselling, or occult sciences.

Ninth House Lord in Third House: An individual's communication style and interactions with siblings may be influenced by philosophy, spirituality, and higher learning as a result of this placement. They may have a desire to communicate their beliefs or cultural knowledge and may excel in fields such as teaching, publishing, or long-distance travel.

Tenth House Lord in Third House: An individual's communication style and networking abilities may be influenced by their career aspirations and public image. They may possess a strong drive to achieve their goals and exhibit excellent leadership qualities, particularly in roles that involve communication and negotiation. Additionally, they may value their reputation and social status highly.

Eleventh House Lord in Third House: People with this placement might greatly emphasise social relationships and networking.

- They could have an extensive network of friends and acquaintances, and show exceptional performance in group settings or social movements.

- It is possible that they also hold an interest in technology or unconventional methods of communication.

Twelfth House Lord in Third House: It's important to keep in mind that this particular placement might cause a person to lean towards a more introverted or private way of communicating with others. They might prefer having alone time or keeping their interactions with others private and may be drawn to discussions surrounding spirituality or metaphysics. Additionally, they could have a communication style that is empathetic and compassionate. The following are descriptions of the different placements of the House Lords in the Third House and how they could potentially impact a person's networking abilities and communication style.

Dasha

The third house lord's Dasha can aid in developing communication skills, allowing individuals to communicate more proficiently, articulately, and convincingly. This can be an advantageous period for those pursuing careers that require excellent communication skills, such as sales, teaching, writing, or speaking. People looking to improve their communication abilities to reach personal or professional goals can also benefit from this period.Strengthened Sibling Relationships: The Dasha of the third house lord can strengthen the bond between siblings or cousins. Relationships may improve, leading to more frequent communication, collaboration, or involvement in joint ventures. However, issues related to siblings may arise during this period, requiring attention and resolution.

The third house lord's Dasha has the power to instill courage, confidence, and a proactive mindset towards life. This particular period could make individuals more capable of taking the initiative in various areas of their lives, leading to greater self-reliance. People might find themselves more willing to explore new opportunities and take risks. This phase can be advantageous for people who aim to develop a more proactive and confident approach towards life. During this time, individuals may feel more confident and inclined to take risks, especially in the areas of communication, education, or short-distance travel.

One may find themselves inclined towards education-related pursuits in the upcoming days. This could involve taking up new courses of study, pursuing intellectual interests, or striving for academic excellence. During this period, there will be a greater emphasis on enhancing one's knowledge and acquiring new skills to broaden one's horizons. It's an opportune time to invest in personal growth and development by dedicating time and effort towards educational endeavours.

During this Dasha, a person may feel a stronger desire to go on shorter trips, either for leisure or work-related purposes. Within this period, there may also be an uptick in local travel, such as visiting family or completing errands. Additionally, individuals may find themselves travelling for educational reasons, such as attending workshops or seminars to gain new skills or knowledge. There may also be opportunities for business-related travel, such as meeting clients or attending conferences.

The placement of the third house lord, along with the Dasha period, has the potential to stimulate an individual's creative and expressive abilities. As a result, they may develop a newfound interest in exploring different forms of artistic expression, including writing, storytelling, painting, or music. Participating in such activities can bring a sense of joy and fulfilment, especially when sharing their ideas and talents with others.

During this period, communication problems with others, such as siblings or neighbours, can occur. These issues might require you to take effective steps to resolve conflicts, misunderstandings, or disagreements. Developing your diplomacy and negotiation skills can help you navigate such situations successfully.

During this time, you may have the opportunity to engage with new people and establish significant relationships. Making new acquaintances or strengthening existing friendships may expand your social circle. Your networking endeavours could also result in exciting personal and professional opportunities. Therefore, take advantage of this period and enjoy the advantages of socializing and cultivating connections!

Individuals who are interested in entrepreneurial ventures related to communication, writing, or technology may experience significant progress and success during the Dasha of the Third House lord. This period can provide an excellent opportunity for them to explore new projects, seek potential partnerships, and engage in marketing and promotional activities to enhance their reach and influence in the market. With their heightened skills in creativity and communication, these individuals may excel in their respective fields and achieve their goals with ease during this phase.

The individual may demonstrate adaptability and flexibility in various situations, particularly those requiring quick thinking and resourcefulness. They may excel in multitasking, problem-solving, and handling diverse responsibilities effectively. These are general tendencies associated with the Dasha of the third house lord in Vedic astrology. The specific outcomes can vary based on the individual's birth chart, the influence of other planetary periods (Dashas), and the ongoing transits. Consulting with a knowledgeable astrologer can provide deeper insights into the potential effects of this period and guidance on navigating its energies effectively.

The Dasa of a planet in Vedic astrology refers to a time cycle that is governed by that particular planet. It is important to consider the implications of both the third house and the house governed by the other planet when examining the outcomes of the Dasa of the third house lord (lord of the third house) in conjunction with the lord of different houses. The following is a comprehensive overview of the potential outcomes when the Dasa of the third house lord is combined with the lords of different houses:

When the Dasa of the Third House Lord corresponds with that of the First House Lord, it has the potential to positively impact an individual's ability to express themselves, communicate effectively, and take initiative. This combination may result in an increase in self-confidence and assertiveness when pursuing personal goals and objectives. As a result, individuals may find it easier to articulate their thoughts and ideas and may be more inclined to take the lead in various pursuits. Overall, this alignment is considered favourable and can empower individuals to reach their full potential in various aspects of their lives.

If the Dasa of the Third House Lord coincides with that of the Second House Lord, it is highly likely that the individual will concentrate on financial matters and communication. During this period, the person may show an increased interest in making profits through communication-related ventures or may focus more on managing finances efficiently by using effective communication skills. The person may find themselves particularly skilled at using language, writing, or other forms of communication to raise their income or manage their expenses. This period's energy and focus can be utilized to achieve a range of financial objectives, whether through entrepreneurial ventures, investment strategies, or other approaches.

During the Dasa period of the third and fourth houselords, individuals tend to focus on family communication and domestic affairs. This phase may involve the individual in activities related to communicating with family members or dealing with property matters. Therefore, it becomes necessary for the individual to concentrate on maintaining healthy relationships within the family and finding solutions to any property-related issues that may arise.

During the period of the Third House Lord's conjunction with the Fifth House Lord, a person's creative abilities, education, and ventures involving speculation may be enhanced. This combination can have a positive influence on communication-related fields, including education, entertainment, and creative pursuits. With the right amount of focus and effort, the person may excel in these areas during this period.

If the third house lord and the sixth house lord are together, it may indicate that the natives are focused on their health, service, and communication skills. With this combination, the individual may be good at addressing issues related to health, service, or conflict resolution through clear communication. They may be inclined towards service-oriented activities that require them to use their communication skills to help others. In general, this combination highlights the importance of effective communication in solving problems related to health or service.

When the combination of the third house lord and the seventh house lord occurs, it has the potential to significantly alter an individual's focus towards relationships, partnerships, and negotiations. During this period, the person may feel compelled to enhance their communication and maintain harmony with their partners or business associates. Additionally, they may need to pay extra attention to their marriage-related matters. This is a period where the individual may have to establish strong bonds and understanding with their significant others to ensure long-term stability and success.

The Third House Lord's Dasa coincides with the Eighth House Lord's Dasa, it can be a powerful combination that brings about significant transformations in an individual's life. This period may involve deep and intense communication with others or secretive conversations that explore occult or psychological subjects. Although both fascinating and challenging, the energy of this combination requires the person to confront their fears and delve into the depths of their psyche to gain a better understanding of themselves and their place in the world. Despite the potential difficulties, this period can also be incredibly rewarding, presenting opportunities for growth, healing, and self-discovery.

During the Third House Lord's Dasa and the Ninth House Lord are combined, it results in a unique phase of spiritual exploration, academic development, and extensive travel opportunities for the individual. During this period, the person may feel inclined towards engaging in philosophical conversations, discussing religion, or pursuing knowledge and wisdom through education. Furthermore, long-distance travel may be on the horizon, which could allow the individual to explore different cultures and broaden their perspective. Overall, this time can be an exciting and enriching experience for personal growth and self-discovery.

The combination of the Third House Lord's Dasa and the Tenth House Lord can highlight career, public image, and authority. The person may possess exceptional communication skills in their professional environment, assume leadership positions, and handle complicated scenarios involving authoritative individuals. This period presents an opportunity for professional growth and accomplishment, and the individual may advance towards their objectives with remarkable progress..

When the Third House Lord's Dasa coincides with the Eleventh House Lord's Dasa, it can have a significant effect on an individual's life, which can manifest in various ways. One of the most significant outcomes is the increased opportunities for social connections and networking. As a result, people may find themselves more involved in group activities and interacting with friends and acquaintances more often, while also pursuing their goals and desires. This alignment may also bring a heightened sense of ambition and a desire to succeed in one's endeavours. Overall, this combination can be a positive influence on an individual's social and professional life, allowing them to forge new relationships and achieve greater success.

The Third House Lord gets combined with the Twelfth House Lord, which can lead to a change in communication style for the individual. They might become more introspective and turn inward, instead of being outgoing and extroverted. The communication tone may become more hidden or secretive, and they may engage in conversations related to spiritual retreat, meditation, and solitude. Furthermore, they may also participate in activities that involve serving others behind the scenes, without seeking any recognition or attention. The overall outcome of this combination may lead to a more subtle and nuanced communication approach. It is important to bear in mind that these interpretations provide a general overview, and the specific results can vary depending on the strength and placement of the planets involved, as well as other factors present in the birth chart. The significance of Dasa, which refers to the planetary period or time cycle ruled by a specific planet, is emphasized in Vedic astrology.

The outcomes of the Dasa of the third-house lord, in combination with the lord of different houses, can help us gain a deeper understanding of the implications of the third house and the house ruled by the other planet.

Dasa of Third House Lord with First House Lord:

This combination can promote self-expression, communication skills, self-confidence, and initiative, leading to assertiveness in pursuing personal goals.

Dasa of Third House Lord with Second House Lord:

During this period, there may be an emphasis on financial matters and communication. Individuals may focus on earning through communication-related ventures or managing finances effectively using their communication skills.

Dasa Of Third house lord with the fourth house

Communication related to family matters and domestic affairs will likely gain importance. The person may actively participate in activities that involve communication with family members or are related to property matters.

Dasa of Third House Lord with Fifth House Lord:

This period may highlight creativity, education, and speculative ventures. The individual may excel in communication-related fields within education, entertainment, or creative pursuits.

Dasa of Third House Lord with Sixth House Lord:

This combination may draw attention to addressing health, service, and communication-related challenges. Individuals can communicate to resolve conflicts and health-related issues or participate in service-oriented activities.

Dasa of Third House Lord with Seventh House Lord:

During this period, relationships, partnerships, and negotiations may take center stage. Communication within partnerships, business dealings, or marriage-related matters may be the primary focus.

Dasa of Third House Lord with Eighth House Lord:

This period may lead to significant personal growth and deep conversations, including exploration of psychological and spiritual matters.

Dasa of Third House Lord with Ninth House Lord:

This time frame may highlight spiritual pursuits, higher education, and long-distance journeys. The individual may engage in discussions related to philosophical or religious topics, knowledge acquisition, or travel arrangements.

Dasa of Third House Lord with Tenth House Lord:

During this period, emphasis may be placed on career, public image, and authority. An individual may excel in communication within their professional sphere, leadership roles, or dealings with authority figures.

Dasa of Third House Lord with Eleventh House Lord:

This combination may highlight social connections, networking, and aspirations. It could involve communication about group activities, friendships, or pursuing goals and desires.

Dasa of Third House Lord with Twelfth House Lord:

This combination could lead to a more introspective type of communication. The person may engage in communication-related to a spiritual retreat, solitude, or activities that involve serving others behind the scenes.

Yoga Related to the third house

The third house can reveal key positive attributes and successes in certain areas of life through the presence of specific planetary combinations and auspicious Yogas. There are notable Yogas and combinations that involve the 3rd house which are worth considering:

If the Lord of the third house is in a benefic navamsa and is being aspected by or conjoined with benefic planets, and Mars is occupying benefic signs, then the Parakrama Yoga is formed. This means that the native will be extremely brave in their life and possess a lion's heart. People may try to harm or discourage them in their personal or professional lives, but they never back down when they have made up their minds. However, they are not stubborn and know when to back down from something. They have the courage to stand up for their beliefs and protect others. But, it is important to be careful, as this courage should be used in the right field and situation.

If Mercury and the Sun unite in the 3rd house, it forms a powerful Budha-Aditya Yoga. This yoga has the potential to significantly enhance communication skills, thereby making the individual highly articulate, intelligent, and capable of achieving great success in areas that require strong communication abilities. This combination is believed to bestow upon the person a sharp intellect, excellent memory power, and exceptional public speaking skills. It is also said to help develop a positive and assertive personality, allowing the person to communicate their ideas and thoughts effectively. Overall, the Budha-Aditya Yoga is considered a highly auspicious combination in Vedic astrology, one that can bring immense success and recognition to the individual.

Saraswati Yoga is a highly auspicious celestial event that occurs when the planets Mercury, Venus, and Jupiter are positioned in either the angular houses (Kendra) or the trine houses (Trikona) from the Ascendant. Additionally, the Yoga is formed if these planets are found together in the 3rd house. This Yoga is considered highly beneficial as it is known to bestow upon individuals great intellectual abilities, artistic talents, and a remarkable command over language. This celestial event is believed to bring immense blessings to those who experience it.

Vasumati Yoga is a planetary combination that occurs when the benefic planets are located in the Upachaya houses, which are the 3rd, 6th, 10th, and 11th houses from either the Moon or the Ascendant. This combination is believed to bring success in ventures and financial prosperity, particularly if the 3rd house is involved. This yoga is considered to be auspicious and is thought to have a positive influence on an individual's life.

The position of benefic planets in the 1st, 3rd and 11th houses, along with their exaltation, ownership, or presence in friendly signs, is considered favourable in astrology. Your chart shows the presence of the **Kurma Yoga**, indicating that you will achieve a high level of fame nationally and internationally. You value your enjoyment and consider it a precious thing, akin to royalty. Your inner personality is characterised by a strong sense of righteousness and a deep belief in the importance of ethics. You are courageous and brave enough to stand up for yourself and others. You prioritise happiness in your life and don't let anything get in the way of that. Additionally, you have a natural leadership ability and a mild temperament that sets you apart from others.

According to your astrological chart, the Sun is in the 10th house and the lord of the 10th house is in conjunction with Saturn in the 3rd house, which indicates the presence of **Ravi Yoga** in your chart. This Yoga suggests several positive attributes about you as a person. You are highly respected by everyone, including those in positions of authority and power. You are well-educated, particularly in the field of science. You gained a lot of fame after turning 15 and will continue to do so in the future. In terms of your personality, you are passionate about everything you do, but you prefer a simple lifestyle and diet. Your physical attributes include lotus-like eyes and a well-developed chest.

Disease-related to Gemini and Mercury

Diseases related to the chest, Nerves, naval, nose, skin, spinal system, and brain nerves, Colds, asthma, bronchitis, Esnophelia, Influenza, T.B., Shoulders, and arms are affected. The third connection with the fourth gives breast cancer, throat-related issues, thyroid issues, deafness, and all kinds of Respiratory system issues.

Mercury affliction with Rahu mars Ketu causes cancer-related issues in the tongue, mouth, and throat. Mercury also causes infections of the tissues, fibres, and cells.

Bones Related to : Metacarpal,Carpal,Ulna radius,Humerous scapula,Upper ribs.

Arteries hold by Gemini : Right and left Bronchites intercostal brachial subclarius redials and ulnars

Veins : Thymus mediotinium,Pulmonary subclavians, Basilic and azygos

Remedies :

The BPHS provides a comprehensive guide to counteract negative influences and enhance positive ones. These remedies, such as chanting mantras, wearing gemstones and yantras, engaging in regular charity and donations, performing yantra worship, conducting homes (fire rituals), performing yajnas (sacrifices), participating in pujas (worship ceremonies), fasting on certain days and worshipping specific deities, are not just rituals, but powerful tools that can be tailored to your specific needs. Depending on which Rashi falls on the third house, who the lord of that house is, where it is posited, and who are the guests seated there, you can identify what they are demanding and where it is lacking to rectify those things, thereby taking control of your health.

A simple remedy of wearing a thread in your hand according to the signification will be beneficial.Third house always demands self effort,one can do significant to those like :

For Mars wear a red colour thread and go to the gym,

sun wearing copper bangle,Gazing the rising sun,

Mercury: always having a book in hand, helping neighbours,

Venus: wearing silk thread, respect all females around you,

Moon, wearing a silver bangle, distributing sweets,

Jupiter: wearing yellow thread, spreading the knowledge,

Saturn: wearing steel Bangle or keeping your surroundings clean,

Rahu and Ketu: wearing bangles made of gold, copper and silver and feeding birds and sweeps

The Best remedy is to howl with the wind, run with the pack, and live like a wolf. Find solace in solitude and be individualistic.

1 Gratitude: "In every howl, a note of thanks for the hunt."

2. Courage: Fear is temporary, Regret is permanent

3. Patience: Good things come to those who wait, but only what's left by those who hustle."

4. Respect: "Treat others as you wish to be treated."

5. Discipline: "Success is the sum of small efforts repeated daily."

6. Vigilance: "Eyes wide open, ears to the ground."

7. Resourcefulness: "Adapt, improvise, overcome."

8. Persistence: "Fall seven times, stand up eight."

9. Tenacity: "Keep going until the prey becomes the hunter."

10. Self-Reliance: "Master of my fate, captain of my soul."

11. Ambition: "Dream big, work hard, stay focused."

12. Empathy: "Strength without compassion is just brute force."

13. Wisdom: "Experience is the best teacher, but the tuition can be steep."

14. Humility: "The true alpha leads from behind."

15. Resilience: Bend, but never break."

16. Integrity: "Stand tall, even if you stand alone."

17. Purpose: "A wolf without purpose is merely a wandering shadow."

18. Optimism: "The darkest night will end, and the sun will rise."

19. Awareness: "Know your surroundings, know yourself."

20. Legacy: "Leave paw prints of kindness and courage wherever you roam."

Ahum Namah Shivaya

www.ingramcontent.com/pod-product-compliance
Lightning Source LLC
LaVergne TN
LVHW061547070526
838199LV00077B/6939